The Seven Habits of Highly Successful Lodges

A guide to managing Lodges in the 21st century

Tony Harvey

First published 2022

ISBN 978 0 85318 626 7

All rights reserved. No part of this book may be reproduced or transmitted in any form or by any means, electronic or mechanical, including photocopying, recording, scanning or by any information storage and retrieval system, on the internet or elsewhere, without permission from the Publisher in writing.

© A. D. G Harvey 2022

Published by Lewis Masonic Ltd
166 Great North Road, Eaton Socon, St Neots, Cambridgeshire, PE19 8EH

Printed in England

Visit the Lewis Masonic website at www.lewismasonic.co.uk

Copyright
Illegal copying and selling of publications deprives authors, publishers and booksellers of income, without which there would be no investment in new publications. Unauthorised versions of publications are also likely to be inferior in quality and contain incorrect information.
You can help by reporting copyright infringements and acts of piracy to the Publisher
or the UK Copyright Service.

All text is copyright A.D.G. Harvey, who asserts his right to be identified as the creator of the
The Seven Habits of Highly Successful Lodges and the author of this work.

All cartoon illustrations are copyright Gerald Sclater.
The Deputy Grand Master's image and signature are reproduced with his permission.

Contents

Foreword 5
Introduction 7
Chapter 1: The Seven Habits 15
Chapter 2: Membership Myths and Facts 33
Chapter 3: The World of the 21st Century Freemason 71
Chapter 4: We have NOT always Done it this Way 85
Chapter 5: Leadership and Management in the Lodge 97
Chapter 6: Who Decides? 113
Chapter 7: But they Don't Want to Change 125
Chapter 8: Communication is Everything 141
Chapter 9: Culture and Belonging 153
Chapter 10: Planning to Succeed 161
To Summarise 185
Bibliography 195
Acknowledgements 199
The Author 203

Dedication

This book is dedicated to

Diane, my wife, and Caroline, my daughter,
who have shared the light and dark of my chequered existence and have always supported me, without fail.

Foreword

RW Bro. Sir David Wootton
Deputy Grand Master

Strategic thinking in United Grand Lodge of England lays great emphasis on membership of Freemasonry, and it is right to do so. UGLE is a unique combination of leadership and membership; of election and appointment; of command and consent; of hierarchy and grass roots; of centre and local. At its heart is membership: individuals joining together to share their time and energies in living out the principles and values of Freemasonry, none because they have to and all because they want to; and the place where members join together is the Lodge or Chapter.

UGLE, and its Provinces and Districts, produce strategy, instruction, guidance, discussion and all kinds of supportive material and events: none will be fully effective unless they are introduced into and acted upon by individual Lodges and Chapters alongside the practices developed by those Lodges and Chapters on their own initiative. This book is researched and written independently of strategic thinking within UGLE itself by an author who is making an active contribution to one of UGLE's principal initiatives, the Members' Pathway, and who brings to the task his career-long professional knowledge as a leadership and management coach and his experience, and analytical and evidence-based approach, of working with organisations of many kinds including those dependent on voluntary membership, and helping them to develop leadership and management practices which will give their members the best experience from their membership and accordingly promote the health and success of those organisations.

Tony Harvey begins with his "Seven habits….." of the title and goes on to set out today's background both in membership data and in the expectations which men have of organisations they join. He then addresses change, both the willingness and the reluctance to embrace it, and the management of it; leadership, management and decision-making – and deciders – in Lodges; communication, planning and culture in Lodges; and the celebration of achievement. The book takes into account research carried out by UGLE. It emphasises that nothing happens by chance - everything is the result of, and requires, thought and effort – and it points ways to success. Tony explains the thinking behind his recommendations and the book is full of ideas for Lodges doing things better: readers will be equipped to make up their own minds on the ideas which work for them and their Lodges.

This book is timely because of its focus on the practical aspects of the individual Lodge and of membership. I particularly like Tony's image of the leaky bucket: we speak much about engagement and retention of members as well as attraction, and the need to focus on both: pouring new members into the "bucket" is less effective than it should be if the "bucket" is "leaking" existing ones.

Lodges and Chapters, and all members of them, will find much to commend itself to them in this book.

Sir David Wootton
Deputy Grand Master

Introduction

I began studying what makes a Lodge successful back in 2005. At that point, I had been a Freemason for fourteen years and was a Past Master of my mother Lodge, Pioneer Lodge No. 9065 in Derbyshire. I was the Lodge Secretary and was active in several other Orders.

In 2005 the then Provincial Grand Master for Derbyshire invited me to join a new group in the Province. We were charged with investigating struggling Lodges, facilitating their growth, or helping them move gracefully to closure. We were all new to this work and so learned as we went along. Our challenge was, "How can a struggling Lodge reverse its decline and restore itself to health and strength?"

I found my experience as a former Assistant County Commissioner for Development in the Scouts to be very helpful. I knew that we needed historic membership data and demographic information. I knew that we needed to build supportive relationships with Lodges. I knew that we had to offer Lodges some tools so that they could help themselves.

I had also been involved in national membership initiatives in the Scout Association. So, I brought a perspective on volunteering from outside Freemasonry, and an understanding of why people join and remain with membership organisations. These experiences also taught me about the management of change in situations when we must win over "hearts and minds" if we are to progress.

My professional work in leadership and organisational development also helped. I coach executives and facilitate senior management teams through their own strategic planning. This gives me a very relevant skillset and a particular range of tools. Around this time, I also developed and published my own model of leadership and change, the Success Cycle. It offers a practical means of aligning our actions to our vision for the future, so that all our activities and resources are devoted to achieving long-term goals.

In both my professional and volunteer lives I was inspired by Stephen Covey's, *The 7 Habits of Highly Effective People*.[1] This was one of the most popular self-help books of the late 20th century. Covey identified the patterns of behaviour, or habits, most frequently found in people he considered to be most effective, or successful, in life. I had been privileged to share a conference platform with Covey and he was impressive.

I applied Covey's thinking to Lodges. What were the habits or features of those Lodges that seemed to be most happy and successful? I had already visited most of the Lodges within my Province and many much further afield. I was also gaining experience as a Lodge Secretary and had been appointed Provincial Secretary in the Mark. I was in a good position to observe what the strongest, healthiest, and most attractive Lodges had in common.

I put my observations together into my own seven habits of highly successful Lodges and wrote a talk on the subject. I started delivering it to any Lodge that was interested. By this time, I had been appointed the first Provincial Grand Mentor of Derbyshire. I had lots of opportunities to share and test my thinking.

Now, years later, I have a lot more experience under my belt. I have visited, observed, and spoken in Lodges in every Province in England and Wales. I have been to Lodges in many of our overseas Districts and in several other Grand Lodges. I have developed other talks on Lodge and membership development, and I played a key role in producing the Members' Pathway for the United Grand Lodge of England[2]. Lodges have adopted these techniques, created development plans, and successfully revived their fortunes.

All this has taught me that even a struggling Lodge with low numbers and little energy can become a happy and successful Lodge once again.

However, such a Lodge needs to act before its decline reaches the point of no return. It can use the seven habits as a sort of health check, and the Success Cycle as the basis for planning. It can use the Members' Pathway as the tool kit for action. All of this is explained in this book. While that explanation is offered in the context of the Craft, the principles and practices in this book are equally relevant to Royal Arch Chapters and membership units in other Orders, and can be applied with equal success.

One thing I should make clear. None of my suggestions in this book, none of the techniques and approaches I offer, require any change to the fundamental landmarks, precepts, meaning or ritual of Freemasonry. All of what I offer and propose is concerned with the management of our Lodges as membership units in the 21st century. The closest I get to proposing any change to our ceremonies is to suggest we plan and organise them to remove the unnecessary pauses and delays that often rob an occasion of its sparkle.

This book is not a threat to the purpose or practice of Freemasonry. On the contrary, it is designed to ensure that its purpose and practice can continue for at least the next generation and hopefully for very many more.

This book is written for those without a background in management, although those who are trained and experienced managers will find it will help them apply their learning to a Lodge. I have written it to be free from management jargon, while still introducing good practices that feature in good management.

There are some who might say that they come to Freemasonry to get away from work and things such as management. I fully understand that. However, whenever a group of people get together to do something, a level of leadership, organisation, planning, communication, and decision making is necessary. Personally, I think in any volunteer group these things should be done simply and well, rather than poorly. Therefore, the purpose of this book is to help Lodges do these very things simply and well, so that our members – and especially those who are coming into Freemasonry now – can enjoy their Freemasonry and have great experiences of the Craft.

Let's remember that the role of the operative Master Mason was to plan the new structure and to supervise its building. Those of us involved in the running of our speculative Lodges today clearly need to plan and manage its activities.

In this book, I start in Chapter 1 by considering "What is a successful Lodge?" and by outlining and explaining seven habits I have observed so called successful Lodges as having in common. These are all habits that your Lodge can adopt, if it chooses to do so, with some discussion, planning, agreement, and co-ordinated effort.

I then present in Chapter 2 a range of historic membership data and the results of various surveys, to demonstrate that our membership challenge is not simply to find more members. I bust several myths and establish instead membership facts to demonstrate that, if we are to thrive in the future – if our Lodges are to be sustainable and healthy – we need to engage and retain far more of the members we introduce. If we stand any hope of achieving this, we must deliver what incoming members seek and we must satisfy their expectations.

In Chapter 3 I share my observations of the lifestyles, experiences, and expectations of those we seek to attract – people whose life and work follow a 21st century mindset. I examine key changes in the world of work since the late 20th century and how they, and other social influences, impact on the mindset, thought processes and expectations of people in their twenties to fifties. Unless we understand these changes, we are unlikely to be able to appreciate and respond to the circumstances in which people live and work today. Based on this understanding, I suggest that our Lodges ought to abandon the "conveyor belts" that so many have created, and which deliver "one size fits all" Freemasonry. Instead, I make a case for them to adopt a more flexible and "member centric" approach, developed around an understanding of the individual.

I developed Chapter 4 around my Cornwallis Lecture, "The future of Freemasonry: evolution and change".[3] I outline how, despite claims that "we have always done it this way", Freemasonry has always evolved and changed throughout its three hundred plus years of organised existence. I then explain why it is necessary for successful membership organisations to continue to evolve and the consequences of not doing so. In fact, I point out how all the United Kingdom's most successful ancient institutions – including the monarchy, the City of London, our oldest universities – have evolved and continued to thrive as a result.

In Chapter 5 I consider the role of leadership and management in the Lodge. I distinguish between these two functions and point out how the various offices fit very well under this distinction. I go further and look at how those in Lodge leadership and management roles may adapt their style to suit circumstances and the members of the Lodge. I finish by suggesting how managing the succession of officer roles and coaching may be used to strengthen the Lodge.

Chapter 6 builds on the previous chapters by clarifying the issue of authority and decision making in the Lodge, and especially where the source of authority lies. I explain how we can build consensus to promote harmony and unity of purpose in a Lodge and I introduce an approach to decision making which promotes both creative and decisive thinking to arrive at better quality decisions.

Based on the understanding we will by now have developed of change, leadership and decision making, in Chapter 7 I offer several techniques a Lodge and its members can use to address resistance to change.

In Chapter 8 I consider why communication is often thought to be one of the major issues in any organisation, including Lodges. I offer an approach to communication that addresses the frustrations we often feel with this issue, and which has been proven to work for all parties, when used properly.

Previous chapters provide the building blocks for the final two. Of these, in Chapter 9 I explain what we mean by Lodge culture and suggest how an understanding of culture can be used to improve the sense of belonging in a Lodge.

Finally, in Chapter 10 I bring everything together by offering an approach to planning, using my Success Cycle model, which unites and aligns our long term hopes and dreams for our Lodge with our day-to-day actions. By following the guidance in this chapter, a Lodge really can implement the lessons learned from earlier ones and truly become a highly successful Lodge.

As you would expect, the summary recaps the key points from the ten chapters. Having read the book, you can use the summary as an aide memoire on your own journey to implement the seven habits.

I do hope this book may inspire in you several thought processes.

First, to have a sense of hope in the "next generation". They may (or may not) be different from yours, but they have the benefit of building on the collective wisdom of their predecessors. Just as their predecessors have, they will tend to make better and better decisions as they develop their own judgement based on their growing experience.

Secondly, recognition of the opportunity we all have – to do something great so that we can pass on to our successors something that is better than when we received it.

Underpinning this is the realisation that our Lodges do not belong to us and none of us as individual members have any more rights over them than any others. We are only the guardians and stewards of our Lodges, safeguarding – and hopefully improving – them for future generations.

Finally, I ask you to sense the direction of travel in both the outside world and in Freemasonry. Very few of us are likely to be able to change this direction of travel. Instead, what we can do is ride the wave it creates. We can anticipate it and do our very best today to secure a good future for our Lodges and their members.

I hope what follows in this book will help you do exactly that.

---

[1] Covey, S.R. (1989) "The Seven Habits of Highly Effective People", Simon & Schuster, London.
[2] See https://b.ugle.org.uk/membership/members-pathway
[3] Awarded by the Provinces of East Kent and West Kent in 2018

Chapter 1

The Seven Habits

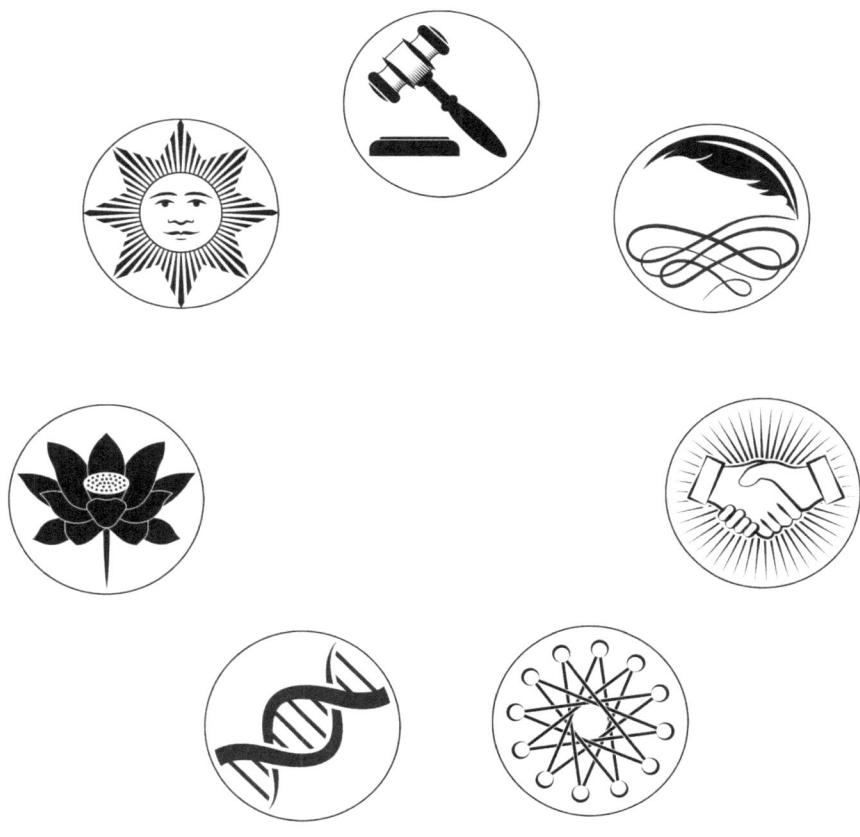

A reflection

I am going to ask you to do something you probably are not expecting. In a minute or so I will ask you to close your eyes.

When you do, I want you to remember your happiest Masonic meeting. It need not have been the grandest or most significant in your journey. The key word is happiest. Recall as much of it as you can. Rewind your memory's video recording of the occasion and play it back in your mind. From the beginning through to the end. As you recall each event, capture key moments like a series of snapshots to remind yourself why it was so happy.

Ok, close your eyes now and take as long as you like. When you have recalled as much as you can, open your eyes again and continue reading.

I have no idea what memories that brought to your mind and I would not want to presume. However, I would like to share with you my memories of a very happy Lodge meeting.

I chose to recall a recent meeting of Walesby Forest Lodge No. 9674, the Scouting Lodge in the Province of Nottinghamshire. I am privileged to have been a founder and I am a Past Master. The meeting was an ordinary meeting. We Initiated a local Scouter, a young man in his early thirties.

As normal, we gathered early and began chatting as different officers went about their preparation. Meeting only five times a year, there were a lot of happy faces as we caught up on Masonic, Scouting, family and other shared interests. The Secretary, Paul, checked that individuals were all lined up to do their various tasks, such as proposing or seconding motions. The Treasurer, Graham, sat collecting dining fees from those of us who hadn't paid in advance. The Director of Ceremonies, John, rehearsed the Deacons and others. In the bar area a group were sitting with the candidate, who was smiling if apprehensive. His proposer introduced me to him just before we all went to put on our regalia.

The meeting flowed well with a relaxed but dignified atmosphere. The Master, using the expanded Pedestal Agenda provided by the Secretary and Director of Ceremonies, presided over all the business with an apparent confidence, despite never having been in such a position before the current year. The occasional witticism punctuated the formality and there were smiles in all quarters of the temple, including from the regular visitors.

The ceremony itself was a joy to see. It was not exactly a demonstration ceremony. Only Josh was word perfect, but that was no surprise! The few prompts were delivered by the Immediate Past Master to the Master and the Assistant Director of Ceremonies to everyone else. They were given in a supportive manner, unobtrusively and without interrupting the flow. It was clear that everyone had prepared well; they knew what they were doing, and the rehearsal and camaraderie meant that teamwork was evident. The Candidate adjusted very quickly to his new status as an Initiate and seemed absorbed in what was happening around him. When he was eventually sat next to the Senior Deacon, clutching his collection of books, letters and brochures, he had a broad smile on his face. Around him his friends expressed their welcome with a range of non-verbal gestures. Those of us nearby reached over to congratulate him.

The administrative part of the meeting had clearly been planned in advance. Those designated to propose and second motions did so without prompt and the Master despatched the votes with a rehearsed ease. The Secretary summarised key communications in the Risings, referring to others having been circulated in advance to all members. The administrative part of the meeting was over in less than five minutes. We were able to move effortlessly to the close of the Lodge and the final procession, which was characterised by smiles. I escorted the new Brother from the meeting so that he would not be left alone and so that he could accept the congratulations from everyone as they came out.

After twenty minutes of busy chatter and laughter in the bar we were called to the Festive Board by the sound of the gong. With the seating plan having been displayed from before the Lodge opened, most of us went straight to our seats where the first course was waiting. The Director of Ceremonies called us to order to receive the Master and Initiate and we stood as the Chaplain read grace before taking our seats in a new hub bub of excited chatter. Just under ninety minutes later we joined in the final strains of the Tyler's Toast and filed out to the bar. We had enjoyed three courses and the usual speeches, toasts, songs and responses. All had flowed one into the other without pause and without the Director of Ceremonies moving from his position immediately behind the Master.

Walesby Forest meetings are often followed by an extended and relaxed gathering in the bar. Here our friendships are deepened as we mercilessly rib each other about some aspect of the meeting. For our newest members, this is the final and most informal stage of their introduction to "Walesby Workings". It is probably best if I leave this happiest of meetings there and return to the here and now. If you wish to experience Walesby Forest for yourself, you are very welcome to visit.

What exactly is a happy and successful Lodge?
Each of us will have our own special reflections on happy Lodge meetings. If you are in any doubt why happiness is so important, let me remind you of part of the Address to the Brethren. It is delivered at every Lodge's Installation Meeting:

> *"I therefore trust that we shall have but one aim in view, to please each other and to unite in the grand design of being happy and communicating happiness."*

Clearly a happy Lodge is one in which everyone is feeling happy and communicating happiness. Being happy means that we are enjoying ourselves, together. This sense of happiness is inclusive; it is no good if some are happy and not others.

Such happiness is not automatic. Many brethren carry with them concerns, anxieties and other emotions. For them, Freemasonry is a "safe retreat of peace and friendship" from the "busy world". But to set aside our worldly baggage, so that we can experience the best of what a Lodge has to offer, requires the Lodge to engage our attention. This is exactly what a happy and successful Lodge does so well.

So, what do I mean by the term "successful Lodge"?

By successful I mean a strong, healthy and attractive Lodge that has good prospects of continued viability.

To me, a strong Lodge is one that has members who are *able* and *willing* to take on all the various offices.

Ability is not an innate quality. It has to be learned and developed. However, new members come to us with existing skills and aptitudes that can be developed so that they become a capable Lodge officer. For example, an experienced administrator may make a good Secretary. A person with an air of authority or presence and an understanding of ceremonial may make a good Director of Ceremonies. A caring and patient person may make a good Almoner or Mentor. An enthusiastic salesperson may make a good Charity Steward.

Willingness is related to our interests, aspirations and motivation. A willing Lodge officer is more likely to do their job well, with energy and enthusiasm. One who is coerced may do it begrudgingly and without conviction. They are more likely to make errors or omit to do key tasks. If we can match Lodge offices to individual members' interests and aspirations, we are more likely to harness the energy that only willing volunteers can inject into their work.

Lodges need to plan ahead if they are to secure a succession of skilled and willing officers. It takes time to learn a new role, to understand what is required of us and to transfer existing skills to a new situation. It is made easier if we can first act as an understudy to another capable officer who is willing to share their wisdom and experience.

By healthy Lodge I mean one that has a continued supply of suitable candidates, a number of members who are developing in Freemasonry and a choice of people for the various offices. The purpose of a Lodge, implicit in the wording of its warrant, is to make Masons. Lodges that cannot find candidates are not fulfilling that purpose. Lodges which have to coerce members to take on offices are likely to feel bad about themselves, become apathetic and go into decline.

An attractive Lodge is one that draws people to it, that existing brethren want to visit, and potential members want to join. What sort of Lodge does that? One that promises and delivers an enjoyable experience that people want to repeat.

Put all these qualities together – strong, healthy and attractive – and you have a Lodge that has a better chance than many to have a sustainable future.

How does a Lodge become happy and successful?

Most Lodges at some time have been happy and successful, even if only in their early days when enthusiastic founders provided the initial energy. Some Lodges sustain their happiness and success over time. Others refresh it by evolving their practices. Sadly, others just seem to lose their "mojo".

The latter either decline until closure or amalgamation, or they take some action to arrest the decline and rebuild or redevelop the Lodge and its fortunes.

What action can such Lodges take? I would start with a review of the Lodge to compare it against the seven habits. An honest review, to which all members contribute, will produce the best results. I would follow the review with the agreement of a plan to evolve the Lodge so that it gets closer to the framework provided by the seven habits. These points are well covered in the Members' Pathway, United Grand Lodge of England's framework and guidance for Lodges to develop their membership.[1] I offer further support for the review and plan process in the following pages.

What are the seven habits of highly successful Lodges?

1 Great ritual and ceremonial

All the meaning of Freemasonry – its core or essence – is contained in the ritual, and in our interpretation of it. Everything else – our rules, ranks and routines – just wraps around the ritual and the lessons it contains. The former is what makes Freemasonry timeless and enduring. The latter evolve and change with each generation. At least they should.

Well delivered ritual allows its meaning to be communicated and interpreted. It helps us to gain the personal insights that are so important for our understanding. Through contemplation of the ritual we grow as Masons and as people.

Ritual delivered in a meaningful manner is most appreciated by the candidate. If it flows well – with supportive rather than zealous prompting, where necessary – it is likely to leave a lasting impression. Such ceremonial work sets standards that new members aspire to emulate. It also attracts visitors to the Lodge.

In contrast, slow, faltering or hesitant ritual becomes uncomfortable for those doing the work. It becomes embarrassing and confusing for those on whom it is being inflicted. Multiple and intrusive prompts interrupt the flow, reducing confidence and exacerbate the problem.

By well delivered ritual I do not necessarily mean perfect ritual. We are not Shakespearean actors, or at least most of us are not. Some brethren (I think again of Josh) can achieve word perfect delivery. However, a requirement that we should all do so creates unreasonable expectations. It results in stress and a loss of confidence. Such a requirement might even turn our attention away from the meaning.

The delivery of ritual is intended to be the communication of meaning from an experienced Freemason to a candidate and to stimulate their search for understanding. When done well, it is personal instruction, not a theatrical performance. It is certainly not intended to be a proud ego trip of self-gratification on the part of the ritualist.

Achieving a high standard of ritual and ceremonial work requires commitment from everyone involved. Senior officers ought to set a standard and an example. The Director of Ceremonies needs to plan ahead and prepare himself and others. Everyone needs to do their best.

It helps if the officers can develop a team spirit. Newer members will need help and encouragement to learn the ritual. Rehearsals – or Lodges of Instruction – will need to be held at regular intervals. Inexperienced ritualists may need help with exactly "how to learn". Rote learning is no longer part of the school curriculum and so many recent Freemasons will be unfamiliar with the technique.

All support and instruction should be given in a friendly and supportive style. Today successful and effective Directors of Ceremonies and Preceptors are coaches rather than disciplinarians. I have seen a Senior Warden, a successful local businessman, walk out of a rehearsal, never to return to the Lodge, after a Director of Ceremonies spoke to him in an aggressive and patronising manner.

The rewards are evident. Lodges that achieve such standards of ritual and ceremonial – and which foster teamwork – do succeed in attracting members who are willing to put in the effort.

The image I have chosen to represent great ritual and ceremonial is the "Master's Gavel" This evokes for me the dignity of ceremonies, the gavel prefacing significant words and actions, and a fresh communication from the Master to the officers and the candidate. When used sparingly but decisively (and, hopefully, not unnecessarily loudly or forcibly) it also links well with another habit.

2 Good management

Good management involves having clear and agreed goals, planning ahead, carrying out those plans and delivering results. My Success Cycle model (see Chapter 10) offers a simple framework for this.

The managers in the Lodge are the heads of the administration team, the ceremonial team, the care team and the fundraisers. That is, the Secretary, Director of Ceremonies, either the Almoner, Membership Officer or Mentor, and the Charity Steward. In successful Lodges they all work together so that the leader – the current Master – can shine.

For the Lodge to work effectively, these managers need to be capable, available and committed. I have already suggested the Lodge should seek members who are able and willing to fill the various offices. In my experience, successful Lodges prioritise these management roles and appoint the best people available. This forms a strong management team. The managers in turn then find others to work with them. Assistants and others can share the workload while learning. They may be the eventual successors to the current office holder.

It helps if these managers can plan the year ahead with the incoming Master, well before the Installation. This requires teamwork. This is a word we haven't traditionally used much in Freemasonry, but which is a byword in other successful organisations. By working together, focused on the same goals, the heads of the four teams can ensure all Lodge activities are well planned, co-ordinated, and executed.

Individual meetings also need planning and co-ordination between the four managers if they are to flow smoothly and be enjoyable. If you took all the ceremonial away from a traditional Lodge meeting you would be left with something very close to a

Victorian committee meeting. No other organisation that I can think of still runs its business meetings in such a time-consuming manner. Today's working Masons do not give their leisure time to take part in lengthy and protracted administrative processes. These can detract from the enjoyment of an otherwise good Lodge meeting.

In successful Lodges, the managers do not consume a lot of time in the Lodge meeting itself. Most of their work is in the background or away from the meeting. On the day of the meeting their job is to make the Master shine. After all, Lodge management is not the reason we join Freemasonry and it ought not detract from the ritual and its meaning. What administration must be conducted can be dispatched quickly and efficiently if planned in advance. As for reading every communication or report, the need for that disappeared with the invention of the Banda machine.[2] Today, technology affords us much more effective methods of keeping people informed.

All of this means having the best people possible in the Lodge's key management roles. This is rarely achieved simply by asking for volunteers. To get the best, you have to invite the best. Successful Lodges create succession plans and discuss them openly and transparently. Everyone then knows what roles will be available and when. Those who wish to express an interest can do so. Everyone will know who is being considered and, ultimately, who will be appointed.

Finally, management systems, processes and tools are constantly changing. A successful Lodge updates its management practices at intervals, to keep pace with the changing expectations of members, and likely future members.

The image of the "Pen" represents good management. Whatever management role we have, whether we are dealing with people or tasks, we communicate through words. The pen suggests we have given our words careful consideration by writing them before we speak or send them.

3 Active support for newer members

The lifestyle and cultural experiences of those joining the Craft today is very different from those in even the recent past.

The 21st century working Freemason has far more leisure options available to them. They are more involved in the home and in bringing up the family. They are more answerable to their family as to how they spend their time and money. They are less deferential to others and much less likely to comply with instructions issued from more senior Freemasons. They want to understand what they are being asked to do, and why. They want to be valued, included, and respected.

If they feel their time is wasted, they may decide to leave. If they feel they are treated as "ceremony fodder" rather than as an individual, they may decide to leave. If they do not enjoy their Freemasonry, if it lacks meaning for them, they may decide to leave.

Nationally, one in every five new members under the United Grand Lodge of England resigns before being presented with their Grand Lodge certificate. When a person outside of the Lodge asks why, many of these brethren cite these very reasons. Rarely do they explain this to their Lodge, however. Many just prefer to give a safe, neutral and inoffensive reason, such as changes in their circumstances.

Masonic Mentoring is about providing active support for newer members. Its purpose is to help them to make sense of the Craft, to learn about its symbols, teaching and customs, and to grow in their enjoyment and commitment. It is more than the passive or reactive approach of simply being friendly and available. To be effective, mentoring has to be planned and organised. This requires time to be invested by the member and their personal mentor. The latter's role is to provide the new member with the information, contact & support they want. It is not simply to educate or instruct them in what the Lodge thinks they should know. The end result of successful mentoring is a happy, engaged and committed member.

The Members' Pathway provides a structure, a process and guidance for this planned mentoring. The document "Briefing the candidate for Initiation" helps the sponsor or personal mentor prepare the candidate. The thread "Support New Member", and in particular the document "Stewardship", outlines an approach for planned mentoring. The document "Personal learning" does the same for the continued mentoring of a member once they have taken all three degrees. There is no longer any reason to leave this essential support for our new members to chance.

By welcoming, befriending and nurturing our newer members we can provide good membership experiences, keep their interest and foster their commitment. After all, these are the brethren who will lead Freemasonry in the future.

The image of the "Handshake" represents an initial welcome, and so much more. When we shake hands, we are greeting each other as equals. We are valuing the other person. We are well placed to build a friendship that is supportive and meaningful to both parties. A handshake is also an action, just as the support we give to newer members must be active, the result of a conscious effort on our part.

4 Engagement of all members

In a more deferential age, members may have been happy to wait until they were senior enough to have an active role in the Lodge and to have a say in its decisions. Many members joining today take the view that their talents should be used and their voice heard. They consider that their membership fee entitles it to be so.

Some Lodges now open Lodge committee meetings to all members, even if not all attendees have full voting rights. This has the obvious advantage of increasing the understanding of all present. New brethren get a better insight into Lodge management. Committee members get a better understanding of newer members' views.

Other Lodges involve newer members, and sometimes their partners, in organising social events. One of my Lodges set up a social committee comprising an even number of members and partners. This has the advantage of using a wider pool of skills and experiences for the benefit of the Lodge. It also helps build relationships with partners and has the potential to attract potential members from a larger network of contacts.

Once a member has been through the chair, are they still engaged in the work of the Lodge? Finding a role for every Past Master keeps them engaged and maintains their attendance. It doesn't have to be a collared office. It just has to use that Past Master's skills and suit his interests and commitment.

Passing on key offices to recent Past Masters also keeps the Lodge refreshed and ensures there are competent people to run it. I was amazed when visiting one Lodge a little while ago to see that none of the recent Past Masters had a continuing office within the Lodge. Not one of those who had been installed in the last ten years wore an officer's collar. Although many were still members, very few were in attendance.

How can such Lodges expect to retain the interest and attendance of Past Masters? What connection do such Past Masters feel with their Lodge? I very much doubt they feel wanted or involved. How can a Lodge expect to have a future if it does not pass on offices from experienced to newer members while the experienced ones are still around to support them?

Family involvement is also increasingly important, especially in social activities. A Lodge that is family friendly is likely to find members' families give more support to their Masonic involvement. In turn, the members can give more time to the Lodge. Those which are not family friendly may well find their activities clash with their members' other priorities.

Creating opportunities for partners and families to be involved also builds their support for Freemasonry in general and gives them an insight into its relevance and meaning.

The image I have chosen to represent this habit is the "Network." Every member of the network is connected to each other. Whatever position a member has in the network, they are all important to the existence and functioning of the network itself. The whole becomes something in its own right, greater than the sum of its parts. So it is with a Lodge. We want all members to be engaged, in a manner that suits their interest and commitment. Indeed, this image also evokes for me the Entered Apprentice's Chain, in which we learn of the importance of each member.

5 Distinctive features that evolve

Lodges that have distinctive features, or which occupy a niche or associate with another organisation, tend to be more successful at attracting new members. Distinctive features might include special Lodge traditions or practices. Niche Lodges include those that meet in the daytime, to attract those who are unable or unwilling to go out in the evenings. Affinity, or special interest, Lodges cater for members with a shared interest. These might be a particular school, university, unit of the armed services, Scouting, Round Table, historic re-enactors, classic cars, and so on.

However, it is not enough just to create such distinctive features and associations. Features that appeal to one generation may not to another. Or they may clash with their lifestyles. Such features must evolve to stay relevant in the context of the world outside the Lodge.

Throughout its history, Freemasonry (and its longer-standing Lodges) has continually evolved and changed. "We have always done it this way" is simply not true. Evolution allows organisations, including Lodges, to stay fresh, attractive and relevant. Traditional organisations, such as the monarchy, the City of London and our oldest universities, have learned this lesson. They recognise they must evolve their internal organisation to synchronise or mesh with the outside world. Otherwise they would become disconnected and irrelevant. They would be unable to engage support or attract and retain members.

Over the years many Lodges have moved away from their founding purpose or origins. For example, many Lodges established to serve particular communities have converged into larger Masonic centres. Others have found that the shared interest they served – such as a school, regiment or hobby – no longer exists or has fallen in popularity.[3]

Unless such Lodges evolve to offer something new, distinctive and relevant, they become just another Lodge. It is far more difficult to attract new members into such Lodges.

The Members' Pathway encourages Lodges to review their practices and prepare a development plan. This includes identifying where its future members will come from. It also covers how its meetings and practices will attract and retain that membership. This process helps a Lodge to evolve, to refresh, to identify specific groups of potential members and to build relationships with affinity bodies.

It is important to discuss the evolution of the Lodge and proposed changes with all members. Some brethren may oppose or resist the proposals. Understanding their concerns and perspective, and agreeing a shared purpose and direction, can help resolve such differences. Ultimately, what matters is to keep the Lodge members working together.

What do you see in the image for this habit? Do you see the double helix of DNA? Or do you see the winding staircase of the second degree? The "DNA strand" represents our distinctive features, our uniqueness. DNA also evolves, allowing new combinations to suit new circumstances. The new Fellow Craft is instructed to climb the "Winding staircase", so that he can receive his wages as a qualified Craftsman. Successful Lodges harness the skills and qualities of its members to allow them to evolve and develop. Both the "DNA strand" and the "Winding staircase" remind me of spirals. These suggest to me that the Lodge has the opportunity to evolve as it progresses round its various cycles. I am thinking especially of the annual cycle of a new Master, the three-to-five-year cycle of a Lodge review and the longer cycle of successive generations of members.

6 *Harmony*

Our ritual teaches us to build and maintain harmony. It is one of the things that sets us apart from other organisations.

Harmony binds a Lodge together and provides a foundation upon which Masonic teaching can come alive.

Equally, nothing destroys a Lodge like <u>dis</u>harmony. New members will soon leave a Lodge that is not practicing its principles of harmonious working. The senior members of a Lodge have a particular responsibility to ensure that harmony is maintained.

One issue that can threaten harmony is the disenfranchisement of newer members from Lodge decision making. When decisions are made by a select few, the other members often feel that their membership is undervalued. In our less deferential age, members are less likely to accept such a situation. They are likely either to challenge it or quietly leave, sometimes without explaining why. In my opinion, it is no longer acceptable that senior members reserve decisions to themselves.

As a Lodge Secretary I always told the incoming Master that leadership and the harmony of the Lodge were their first priorities. I explained they are key to its future success, for their year and beyond.

Consultation and brotherly love are essential for harmony to exist. By consultation, I mean keeping members informed of issues, consulting them on contentious matters, exercising caution with respect to decisions. In this way, everyone has the chance to have their say, be heard and to work happily and willingly together for the collective good.

Brotherly love is built by being together, in labour and refreshment. It is enhanced by supporting each other and by always considering the best interests of the whole. It is strengthened by a balance of Masonic activities and social activities. This bond is destroyed when cliques and factions take over, whether they be based on seniority, other interests or when differences of opinion arise.

Harmony can be threatened by little things and should not be taken for granted. It has to be valued, worked at and constantly refreshed.

The "Lily" and the "Lotus flower" are powerful images for this habit. Lilys thrive almost anywhere and are long lasting. They represent love and devotion. The lotus flower has a unique daily life cycle, disappearing at night into the mud of a riverbed, only to bloom again, fresh and clean, each morning. It endures and is reborn.

It has been adopted by many religions to represent spiritual properties. Achieving harmony requires brotherly love and devotion, represented by the lily. It requires us, like the lotus flower, to overcome any worldly matters which can drive us apart, to endure difficulty and to continue with a focus on something above and beyond us, something that is worthy and precious.

7 Leadership, energy and enthusiasm

Leadership and enthusiasm provide the spark that breathes life into the other six habits. Energy provides the motive force to move and function well.

What is the difference between leadership and management? Leaders communicate a way forward in such a manner that others will willingly follow. Managers use structured methods to plan and organise so that things are done in a timely and correct manner. Both are necessary. If a Lodge is to be successful, the leader and the managers should work together.

Good leadership provides a Lodge with purpose and direction. If leadership and management were a bicycle, leadership would be the handlebars and front wheel while management would be the peddles, gears and rear wheel. The bicycle cannot function without both.

Every Master wants, and deserves, their year to be special. The annual cycle of a new Master, supported by good management teams, balances the fresh approach of the new with continuity from the past. Wise Masters concentrate on providing leadership, leaving others to manage the details of the Lodge.

So, an incoming Master who tells the Lodge that they want an enjoyable year, in which all members will be able to take part, will often provide new impetus to a Lodge. Ideally, the Master will back that up with an announced programme of ceremonial and social events. If they show enthusiasm, involve and value their members and build a team approach to Lodge work, they will gain their loyal and enthusiastic commitment in return.

Enthusiasm is infectious. It sparks enthusiasm in others. A good Master refreshes the enthusiasm of their membership. However, a successful Lodge also has the continued energy that comes from the officers in management roles. Their energy – the peddle power within the Lodge's bicycle – sustains the Lodge and keeps it active. You can feel the energy and enthusiasm in a successful Lodge, just as you can feel the apathy in a Lodge that has run out of steam. The latter feels as if the Lodge has parked its bike against a wall to rust and decay.

The image of the "Sun in splendour" is used in the Grand Master's regalia, clearly to represent leadership. It has been used in many cultures and civilisations to represent life, energy, optimism, joy, and confidence. I can think of no better symbol to represent this habit.

These then are my seven habits of highly successful Lodges. They reflect balance between different aspects of Lodge life; leadership vs management, ritual and meaning vs organisation, the needs and expectations of the individual vs those of the Lodge.

None of these habits are new. None of them should come as a surprise. Collectively they are just my personal top seven, based on my own observations and experience. However, if your Lodge is struggling the list might help you think afresh about your way forward. They may act as a template for your discussions, plans and action.

If your Lodge has reached the point where it cannot practice the seven habits and cannot see a way forward, and if it is anticipating closure, the Members' Pathway offers seven "alternative futures". The sooner you consider these the better the opportunity your Lodge will have of a revived future.

I now want to enlarge on the seven habits, not by looking at them in turn but by examining issues that impact on how we might develop a Lodge and its habits.

Let us start that by looking at membership trends and see if we can bust a few myths along the way.

---

[1] See https://b.ugle.org.uk/membership/members-pathway
[2] "Banda" was the UK brand name for the spirit duplicator, invented by Wilhelm Ritzerfeld in 1923.

[3] For example, the Lodge of Unity Peace & Concord No. 316 – a Lodge formed in 1737 and attached to the 2nd Btn The Royal Scots (The Royal Regiment) – declined after the Regiment lost its identity. It evolved to become the Installed Masters' Lodge for the Kindred Lodges Association and is now thriving.

Chapter 2

Membership Myths and Facts

Most Freemasons are aware that our membership has been in decline for some years. However, in my thirty plus years as a Freemason, I have seen very little awareness, presentation, or analysis of real membership data other than the year-on-year comparisons often produced for annual reports. A small increase one year does not show sustainable growth. It is often followed by a loss the next.

I suspect few members are aware of the duration or extent of our membership decline, or of the trends in our membership figures.

By analysing long term membership data, we can identify such trends. Trends tend to reflect underlying patterns in behaviour. Understanding such trends, and any changes in their direction, help us identify healthy and unhealthy membership practices and allow us to predict future growth or decline.

In the 1980s I was a researcher for the Medical Research Council. I published a number of papers based on my clinical and experimental research. My scientific training taught me to base conclusions on valid and reliable data. I adopt a similar robust approach when researching history. In my opinion, we should base our future plans on an understanding of the past, on current circumstances, on trends and on real data

In this chapter I provide a pool of evidence for us to draw upon. The data forming the pool all relates to the United Grand Lodge of England (UGLE).

The data does not include that from the period of the Covid-19 pandemic. As we are still adjusting to effects of the pandemic, it is too early to analyse and understand its impact on the underlying behaviour of Lodges and changes in membership. To include data from 2020 and 2021 would temporarily distort the underlying trends.

Clearly there were fewer Initiations in that period. However, it appears that the much-feared increase in resignations because of the pandemic has not come about. In fact, early indications are that the annual number of resignations have continued to fall in line with the pre-pandemic trend.

Obviously, the data will become out of date as time progresses. It will soon be overtaken by other events, especially as we see the impact of UGLE initiatives such as the Members' Pathway and the National Digital Marketing Campaign. I believe this book will also make a difference if sufficient Lodges implement the ideas it contains. So, this chapter represents a point in time. I will rewrite this chapter at intervals.

Being a three-hundred-year-old membership organisation, you might think we have rich sources of data available for analysis. In fact, accessing, analysing and interpreting membership data is a major challenge.

In organisations where membership is centrally acquired and managed, data might be available at the press of the return key. However, membership of Freemasonry is acquired bottom-up, through Lodges. The data has to be submitted by local volunteer Secretaries. Some of them are very efficient. Others are less so.

Further, throughout our history membership has been administered using paper. Although today UGLE uses a computerised membership system, until Hermes (the new administrative portal to the membership system, designed for Lodge Secretaries) has been fully implemented it will still rely on paper coming from Lodges. There has always been a time lag between an event occurring in a Lodge and notice of that event reaching UGLE and its databases. Membership data is not yet accessible in real time.

Additionally, Lodge records are not always complete. Lodge minute books are notoriously full of gaps. Lodges have not always recorded the information we would now find useful.

There is also the difference between counting *members* and counting *memberships*. An individual Freemason will count only once as a *member* of UGLE, and of each of their Provinces or Districts. If they are a member of several Lodges, each will increase by one the count of *memberships*. To each of their Lodges, this makes no difference; they are a member no matter what. When that member eventually leaves all their Lodges, either voluntarily or by death, the total number of Grand Lodge *memberships* will be reduced by the number of Lodges to which they belonged.

As a result of these factors, long term analysis of membership data is not the exact science my scientific training craves.

To write the following I have drawn on multiple sources of data. These include:

1 Initiation and Resignation figures for the whole of UGLE for the period from 2010,
2 UGLE's annual Directory of Lodges and Chapters,

3. Lanes Masonic Records,
4. Published and unpublished reports of surveys, and
5. Private correspondence with other researchers.

I am seeking to demonstrate long-term trends and underlying patterns. I have made explicitly clear where, in the absence of data, I have made inferences or assumptions.

Year on year comparisons tend to show occasional "blips". I use the "moving average" technique to overcome these. A "moving average" is calculated by adding up all the data for a specific measure (eg, Initiations) over a given period. For membership data I use a period of five years. Therefore, the "five-year total" for a given year is the sum of specific data for the previous five years. The following year the same calculation is repeated, this time subtracting the oldest figure from six years ago and adding in the newest.

The resulting "moving average" smooths out all but the largest of blips and shows the underlying trend in the data. We can use this to predict future growth or decline by plotting our moving average on a graph. This is because that trend is a result of how the Lodge manages members and memberships over time. The trend will continue until the Lodge makes a substantial change in its practices.

You can combine two five-year totals to calculate "five-year net growth." First, add up the total number of gains in the previous five years. Then add up the total number of losses in the same five years. Next subtract the total number of losses from the total number of gains. The result is "five-year net growth". If the result is negative, it indicates a decline rather than growth. If five-year net growth is getting bigger, the situation is getting better. If it is getting smaller, the situation is getting worse. The next year repeat the calculation and update the graph to show long-term trends.

I have found "five-year net growth" to be the single most useful indicator of whether a Lodge is growing or declining.

UGLE now calculates what it calls the "Membership Challenge" for each Province. This is the "difference between gains and losses of members. It is expressed as percentage of Initiates."[1] Where the number of losses is greater than the number of gains, this measure "identifies the increase in Initiates required in order to stabilise our membership numbers." In practice, the Membership Challenge will most likely be reduced through a combination of increasing gains and reducing losses. I encourage Lodges to calculate their own "Membership Challenge" and use this along with "five-year net growth" as part of their review and analysis of their membership situation.

Let's start with the issue of membership growth or decline, before moving on to other matters.

Membership decline

Every year our Lodges lose more members through resignations than they gain through Initiations.[2]

In the five years to the end of 2019, Lodges under UGLE Initiated 42,519 new Freemasons. In the same five years, there were 57,804 resignations from Lodges

That is a difference of 15,285 more resignations than Initiations. It shows a five-year net growth of -15,285. It is an average of 3,057 more memberships lost than Initiations every year. This is the equivalent of a medium size Province lost each and every year.

If growth came from finding more candidates, our Lodges would have to find 35.9% more Initiates just to stand still. As there has been a slow decline in the number of Initiations for many years, something very significant indeed would have to change for that to happen.

I should point out that these are resignations of individual Lodge *memberships*. Not every resignation is a loss of a *member* to UGLE. At the end of 2019, 21.3% of all memberships were held by brethren who are members of more than one Lodge. The number of *members* was 78.7% of the number of *memberships*.[3]

So, let's assume that, in the five years to the end of 2019, 78.7% of the 57,804 resignations represented the loss of an actual member from UGLE. That would be 45,491 members lost, or an average of 9,098 each year. If our assumption was correct, the revised five-year net growth, based on members rather than memberships, would be -2,972. That would be a net loss of, on average, 594 members each year.

To these losses we should add the number of deaths each year, and the number of exclusions, cessations and expulsions from membership. Deaths

Year ending	No. Lodges	Initiations		Grand Lodge certificates		Resignations		5-year net gain / (loss)	
		No.	5-year total	No.	5-year total	No.	5-year total	Per year	5-year net gain
31/12/2010	7,893	9,286		7,556		12,980		(3,694)	
31/12/2011	7,792	9,198		8,089		13,357		(4,159)	
31/12/2012	7,696	8,850		7,780		13,013		(4,163)	
31/12/2013	7,592	8,379		7,612		12,870		(4,491)	
31/12/2014	7,504	8,570	44,283	7,204	38,241	12,229	64,449	(3,659)	(20,166)
31/12/2015	7,442	8,343	43,340	7,142	37,827	11,836	63,305	(3,493)	(19,965)
31/12/2016	7,368	8,355	42,497	7,056	36,794	11,675	61,623	(3,320)	(19,126)
31/12/2017	7,291	8,639	42,286	6,714	35,728	11,150	59,760	(2,511)	(17,474)
31/12/2018	7,236	8,575	42,482	7,014	35,130	11,653	58,543	(3,078)	(16,061)
31/12/2019	7,175	7,929	41,841	7,483	35,409	10,375	56,689	(2,446)	(14,848)

Table 1: Key membership changes 2010-19

Membership Myths and Facts — 39

	12/31/10 1/1/11	12/31/11 1/1/12	12/31/12 1/1/13	12/31/13 1/1/14	12/31/14 1/1/15	12/31/15 1/1/16	12/31/16 1/1/17	12/31/17 1/1/18	12/31/18 1/1/19	12/31/19
Initiations	9,286	9,198	8,850	8,379	8,570	8,343	8,355	8,639	8,575	7,929
5 yr Initiations	12,980	13,357	13,013	12,870	44,283	43,340	42,497	42,286	42,482	41,841
Resignations	12,980	13,357	13,013	12,870	12,229	11,836	11,675	11,150	11,653	10,375
5 yr Resignations					64,449	63,305	61,623	59,760	58,543	56,689
Net gain / (loss)	(3,694)	(4,159)	(4,163)	(4,491)	(3,659)	(3,493)	(3,320)	(2,511)	(3,078)	(2,446)
5 yr net gain / (loss)					(20,166)	(19,965)	(19,126)	(17,474)	(16,061)	(14,848)

Graph 1: Key membership changes 2010-19

are unavoidable and cannot be managed. Exclusions, cessations and expulsions are relatively small in number.

To be absolutely accurate, we should also add to the gains the number of joining members. These are existing Freemasons who join an additional Lodge. They are already included in the total number of members of UGLE, unless they are unattached and re-joining a Lodge after a period away from Freemasonry.

The addition of a joining member certainly can boost the Lodge they join. However, it does not boost the membership of the Craft as a whole. Equally, whether we talk of members or memberships, every resignation is a loss to a Lodge.

The harsh reality is that the membership of UGLE is in decline. It has been since around 1980. At the end of 1998 UGLE recorded 338,357 individual members. At the end of 2019 there were 188,401.[4] This is a loss of 44.3% of actual members, not memberships. If this continues, and we lose another 44% in the next twenty years, by 2040 Freemasonry will be a shadow of its former self. It will have just over 100,000 members. Many of our 7,080 Lodges[3] will have closed, as will many of of our Masonic Halls. Provinces and Grand Lodge will have had to reduce their fixed costs.

Our 40-year membership decline runs parallel to that reported by other membership organisations, and elsewhere. In his seminal book, "Bowling Alone"[5], the Harvard social scientist Robert Putnam traced the rise and fall of American community engagement in the 20th century. He found a marked generational change in engagement after the post-war baby-boomer generation became adults. From the 1970s to the end of the century, almost all measures of community engagement in the USA – including membership of community organisations – fell by over fifty percent. Knowing we are not alone may be reassuring but it does not help us address the issues we face.

There is some good news. We are actually very good at finding new candidates. We Initiated a total of 86,802 in the ten years to the end of 2019. Each year Initiations run at more than one per Lodge. Over those ten years there was an average of 1.16 Initiates per Lodge each year. However, in five of those ten years the number of Initiations was less than the previous year. The five-year total also shows a fall from 44,283 for the five-years to the end of 2014 to 42,519 for the five years to 2019.

Thankfully, resignations have also been falling over the last ten years, and at a faster rate than Initiations. The five-year total was 64,449 at the end of 2014. It was 57,804 at the end of 2019. In seven of the years between 2011 and 2019 the number of resignations was less than the previous year. For UGLE as a whole, the net difference between Initiations and resignations for the five-year period (ie, five-year net growth) ending 2014 was -20,166. Five years later, at the end of 2019, it was -15,285.

We are still in decline, but we are improving, thanks mostly to resignations reducing in number every year since at least 2011. However, at this rate, it will take around 15 years for five-year net growth to become positive and for membership to start to grow. By then we will be a much smaller organisation. The only way to change this predicted outcome is for more of our Lodges to do something different. Starting now.

Implications for Lodges

The majority of our Lodges know they are in decline. However, many don't seem to recognise the real issue. Some appear to think all they need to do is find the next candidate and their Lodge will be alright. They think they can carry on as they have always done. No need to change anything.

It's rather like wanting to fill a bucket with water when it is riddled with holes. If the bucket leaks water faster than you can pour it in, you will always end up with less than when you started. You will have wasted a lot of water! This is exactly what has been happening to Freemasonry. Over a long period of time resignations have exceeded Initiations. Just think about those 45,000 Freemasons who resigned in the last five years. What are they now telling others about their experience of Freemasonry?

If you plot your Lodge's total number of members for each year you will see how the Lodge is doing. The further you go back the better. If you then plot your Lodge's five-year net growth (or decline) on the same graph, you will see when things have changed. A change in the direction of the graph indicates something that made a difference. You can also extend the graph to predict what the membership will be at particular points in the future, assuming you change nothing.

It all boils down to this. If your Lodge is in decline, you have to act now to identify the cause and take remedial action.

The above figures for Initiations include unsponsored brethren introduced since we became more visible and started promoting Freemasonry on websites and social media. Despite all the success we have had in this area, Initiations are still on a slow downward trend. If we had not been promoting Freemasonry, it is safe to assume many of the members who first approached us may not have joined. Or, if they had, it is likely they would have taken longer to do so. However, doing these things has not been enough to turn decline into growth.

Something more is needed.

An historical perspective

How does our current situation compare with the past? Has Freemasonry always been much bigger? Are we really in trouble now?

It is very difficult to gather reliable historic membership data. For example, the premier Grand Lodge did not introduce individual registration until 1768. Therefore, I have looked at these questions from the perspective of Lodges. I have divided our history into three periods of approximately 100 years each.

According to John Lane[6], a total of 229 Lodges were on the roll of the premier Grand Lodge (the "Moderns") up to 1739. Thereafter that Grand Lodge issued 874 warrants between 1740 and 1813. The "Ancients" Grand Lodge warranted 509 Lodges between 1751 and 1813. Two other Grand Lodges warranted another 14 between them.[7] In total, 1,626 Lodges had been formed or warranted up until the Union of 1813. By 1813, at the time of the Union, there were only 388 Moderns and 260 Ancients Lodges remaining; 978 (60.15%) of all Lodges formed in the previous 100 years had already closed. Only 648 Lodges were still in existence at the birth of the United Grand Lodge of England.[8]

In the eighteenth century, many Lodges lasted a relatively short time.

From the 1813 Union to the end of 1920, 4,187 new Lodges were formed, making a total of 5,813 since 1717. In 1832 and again in 1863, Lodge numbers were "closed up". The last Lodge granted a warrant in 1920 was Purcell Lodge No. 4236, in the Province of Northumberland. By then only 3,612 Lodges were still working, just 62.1% of all those ever founded.

Between 1921 and the end of 2021, a further 5,785 new Lodges were formed, making a total of 11,597 since 1717. The last Lodge issued with a warrant in 2021 was Somerset Military Lodge 10021.[9] At the time of writing, just 7,080 Lodges are still working, 61.1% of all those ever founded.

The last one hundred years has seen the establishment of well over half of all Lodges created. A total of 4,517 Lodge have closed since 1717. Over one third of all Lodges ever founded have since closed.

To summarise the three periods, between 1717 and 1813 1,626 Lodge were formed. In the following one hundred and seven years another 4,187 Lodges were added. In the last one hundred years there have been a further 5,785.

In the thirty years following the Union in 1813 there was no real net growth in the number of Lodges, despite another 356 new warrants having been issued. At the time of the death of the Duke of Sussex in 1843, the number of working Lodges was 654; just six more than at the Union.

In the next thirty years 706 new Lodges were warranted but at the end of 1862 (when UGLE decided to close up the numbers again) only 948 were active.[10]

Since then, UGLE has seen three large increases in membership. Each has prompted the founding of new Lodges.

The first large increase was following the appointment of HRH The Prince of Wales (subsequently HM King Edward VII) as Grand Master in 1875. The next ten years saw 541 Lodges formed, 27.6% of the 1,956 Lodges then working.[110]

The second was following the First World War. Between the end of 1918 and 1928, 1,182 new Lodges were formed, 26.9% of the 4,383 Lodge then working.[12]

The third was following the Second World War. Between the end of 1945 and 1955, 1,214 Lodges were formed, 18.1% of the 6,693 Lodges then working.[13] [14]

When membership was booming, Provincial Grand Masters encouraged brethren to form new Lodges. This was largely so that members did not have to wait a disappointingly long time to become Master. Once a Lodge is in possession of its warrant it is considered to be a "Private Lodge", entitled to manage its own affairs and regulate its own proceedings, providing it complies with the Book of Constitutions.[15] A Metropolitan, Provincial or District Grand Master cannot impose change on a Lodge. They can only encourage struggling Lodges to change direction, adapt to survive or reach the decision to close. That has proved far more difficult to achieve.

At the time of writing, in 2022, we have 7,080 Lodges working under UGLE.[16] This is almost twice as many as the 3,612 in 1920. The total number of members in UGLE at the end of 1920 is estimated to have been around 200,000. At the end of 2019 it was 188,401. So, we have a little fewer members than one hundred years ago but twice as many Lodges. On average, Lodges are half the size they were back then.

The average size of a Lodge is currently 33.4 members.[17] Therefore, around 3,500 Lodges will have less than 30 members. Most Provinces would consider these Lodges to be in the "at risk" category.

To summarise, we have not always been much bigger. On the contrary, we only achieved our peak in the second half of the 20th century. Our current membership compares with that of 100 years ago when we were much more visible and well respected. However, we then had half the number of Lodges. Many current Lodges have less than 30 members. Most

Period	Highest Lodge number at end of period	Increase in number of Lodges	Number of working Lodges
1717-1813	now 339	1,626	648
1813-1920[1]	4236	4,187	3,612
1921-1930	5249	1,013	4,547
1931-1940	5832	583	5,135
1941-1950	7070	1,238	6,341
1951-1960	7756	686	7,008
1961-1970	8371	615	7,499
1971-1980	8980	609	8,074
1981-1990	9414	434	8,469
1991-2000	9738	324	8,656
2001-2010	9864	126	7,893
2011-2020	10005	141	7,233

Table 2: Changes in the number of Lodges since 1717

importantly, our membership has been in decline for 40 years and that decline has not been arrested.

Implications for Lodges

If a Lodge has a declining membership, its situation is likely to get worse unless it does something to change its fortunes. After all, "if you always do what you have always done, you will always get what you have always got". A few new members will not fix a leaky bucket.

Not all of our current Lodges will survive. Evolutionary forces apply as much to Freemasonry and its Lodges as they do to other populations and groups within them. Evolution says that small variations between groups (eg, Lodges) result in some being favoured in the search for resources (ie, potential members) while others fail. Darwin himself said there is, "One general law, leading to the advancement of all organic beings, namely: multiply, vary, let the strongest live and the weakest die".[19]

Our Lodges have certainly multiplied but not all have varied. However, our longest serving Lodges are still with us precisely because they have always evolved. They have adapted aspects of their practices to suit the changing external circumstances. Some traditions have survived as a memoir of the past, but often they have been adapted and given a modern flavour. Of course, new traditions are being introduced all the time.

To arrest a decline in membership, a Lodge should understand why its own bucket is leaking. It can start by analysing the trends in its own membership data and understanding the reasons behind them. It can then take stock of its situation and identify which of its practices are favourable to current and likely future members and which are not. It can make changes to make the Lodge more appealing, attractive and relevant. The Members' Pathway[20] puts into the hands of every Lodge the tools and techniques for completing such a review and for developing a Lodge plan. It also offers successful techniques for attracting, introducing and retaining new members.

Given that almost half of our Lodges have less than 30 members, taking such action is more than important. It is critical to their survival. It may even be critical to the survival of Freemasonry in its current form.

Wider implications

We could consider the late 20th century rise in membership to be like a tidal wave. It created a temporary increase in membership. However, at the time we didn't look at it in this way. We expanded our infrastructure of Lodges and Masonic Halls to meet the needs of a growing membership. We are now left with that legacy. Unless we adjust now, we may find ourselves dragged down by having too many Lodges and costly meeting places being supported by a reducing membership.

Many members look back on the 1970s and 80s as a Masonic golden age, as if those years represented something that should be restored. While our membership peaked then, those years also sowed the seeds of our current difficulties and certainly did not reflect Freemasonry's long history. Over three hundred years the norm has been for:

- Lodges to come and go
- Memberships to be closer to 40-50 per Lodge
- Some members to progress and others not, and
- Those who wish to do so to achieve the chair in less than ten years.

I don't wish to appear negative or pessimistic. I only seek to be realistic. Decline in Freemasonry and its Lodges is not inevitable. We Initiated 86,802 new Freemasons in the ten years to the end of 2019. That is 12.1 per Lodge. People clearly wish to join. If any Lodge has retained every member it Initiated in the last ten years it will probably be growing.

Perhaps a realistic expectation of future goals, if we can arrest and reverse the decline, is:

- Between 200,000 and 250,000 individual members
- Early years loss lower than 10% of Initiations
- Average membership between 40-50 per Lodge, implying
- Around 5,000 Lodges.

To understand why most of our Lodges are not growing requires more than an understanding of the figures. It requires consideration of peoples' experiences, opinions and wishes. I have explained it is difficult to obtain long-term hard (ie, objective and factual) quantitative membership data. Thankfully, there has been some good research into qualitative aspects of membership. There have been properly conducted surveys examining:

1. What people think of Freemasonry
2. Why some join, and
3. Why they either remain or leave.

We also have reports from external surveys looking at why and how people join membership organisations in general.

Unfortunately, the results and implications of all this work have not been widely understood. Many members seem to think growth depends on action from UGLE rather than by members and their Lodges. They believe that if UGLE promotes or markets Freemasonry it will lead directly to growth.

The reality is a little more complex. Nevertheless, once it is understood it gives very clear direction to our attempts to create more strong and healthy Lodges.

Let us start by backing up my claim that people wish to join. First, I will look at data relating to membership organisations in general. Then I will look at that relating to Freemasonry in particular.

The Community Life and Taking Part Surveys

The UK government's Department for Digital, Culture, Media & Sport (DCMS) conducts two surveys into different aspects of volunteering; the Community Life Survey and the Taking Part Survey. Both cover England only. I am going to assume the situation in Wales, the Isle of Man and the Channel Islands is broadly similar to England's.

The results for 2019/20,[21] show that 23% of all adults take part as a member of a club, society or organisation at least once per month. 42% of these are connected to hobbies, social clubs and recreation. This is the closest of the survey's categories under which Freemasonry could fit. This works out as 9.66% of all adults. The suggestion that people don't wish to join membership organisations is not supported by the surveys. Almost 10% do.

If these rates apply to Wales as well as England, it works out as 2.24 million men in England & Wales.[22] We should remove from this figure the 38% who "do not believe in any sort of God(s) or greater spiritual power".[23] This leaves a potential market for male Freemasonry in England & Wales (ie, under UGLE) of 1.39 million.[24] Our current share of this market is around 13.4%, or 0.8% of all adult males in the country.[25]

According to the 2018/19 survey,[26] participation does vary across age ranges. The lowest is 15% for those between 25 and 34 years old. The highest is 28% for those between 65 and 74 years. There is a small difference between those in work (22%) and those who are "economically inactive" (eg, retired) (27%). Only 17% of those who are unemployed take part in membership organisations. One in five (20%) become involved in running the group they joined, including committee work, administration and organising events. Participation in membership or voluntary organisations peaked in 2005 and then declined following the economic crash in 2008. It has now returned to levels very similar to the peak in 2005.

According to the surveys, the following are the top five benefits of belonging to a membership organisation:

1. 'A sense of satisfaction from seeing the results' (97%)
2. 'I really enjoy it' (96%)
3. 'It gives me a sense of personal achievement' (88%)
4. 'Meet people and make friends' (86%)
5. 'Gives me the chance to do things that I am good at' (83%).

If a Lodge is run well, it can deliver all of these benefits, to a high level.

Of course, not everyone wishes to join an organisation. The most common reasons for not doing so were reported to be:

1. 'Work commitments' (53%)
2. 'Other commitments' (37%)
3. 'Home or childcare' (23%).

Finally, 11% did not know of any groups seeking members and 10% did not know of opportunities to join.

Implications for Lodges

These surveys demonstrate that there are plenty of people in our communities who wish to join membership or voluntary organisations. There are more than enough to strengthen our existing Lodges. In addition, Freemasonry is very capable of delivering the satisfaction and personal growth opportunities that joiners seek.

One concern is that only 20% become involved in running their local organisation. Smaller Lodges place a high expectation on members to take office. If this expectation becomes pressure, it may be a factor in our high level of resignations.

Interestingly, many who resign from their Lodge often give the very reasons shown for people not joining in the first place; other commitments. This suggests Lodges should be especially careful to discuss with applicants whether they can make time for Freemasonry around their other commitments.

Given the wide range of opportunities open to men, a 13.4% share of those who join organisations (related to hobbies, social clubs and recreation) looks quite good. This is a very competitive market. If a Lodge is not visible in its local community, men who might otherwise become interested in Freemasonry may well go elsewhere. Given that leisure time is a precious resource, we really have to attract people to us before they find something else instead.

Do we know how many of these 1.39 million men are interested in Freemasonry? One survey from 2012 suggests a good proportion could be.

The Social Issues Research Centre (SIRC) report

In 2012, UGLE commissioned the Social Issues Research Centre (SIRC)[27] to examine the place of Freemasonry in 21st century society. This was the first time UGLE had asked an independent third-party to consider these issues.

SIRC surveyed and interviewed Freemasons and those who are not Masons to find out if Freemasonry is still relevant and attractive. It examined whether a male-only organisation with an emphasis on ritual still had a place in the 21st century.

UGLE summarised the key findings:[28]

"Nearly half (49%) wanted to know more about Freemasonry, while a quarter of male respondents (26%) would consider joining. Of these, 68% were attracted to the idea of belonging to a group and making new friends and 58% would like to do more in the community.

"Of those men who would not consider becoming a Mason, the single biggest response (given by 40%) was the misconception that "it's not for people like me". (Freemasonry is actually open to all – regardless of race, colour, religion, political views or social or economic standing.)

"More than a third (37%) of all respondents said that, if they met someone they knew to be a Freemason, they would be hesitant to raise the subject with them, while a further 20% would definitely say nothing, wrongly believing Masons are not allowed to talk about their membership. (In reality, members are actively encouraged to talk about the organisation and the important contribution it makes to society.)"

SIRC found that:

1. There is a continuing place for single-sex organisations
2. Freemasonry provides a sense of friendship, belonging and structure
3. Our ritual gives meaning to our everyday life.

It concluded that Freemasonry is probably more relevant today than ever before.

In commenting on the report, the then Grand Secretary, VW Bro. Nigel Brown[29], said:

"This report will form an important part of our discussions as to how best to ensure that Freemasonry continues to evolve and adapt to meet the needs of its members and also of wider society, while at the same time retaining the distinctive character and intrinsic values that have attracted members for centuries and continue to appeal to people today."

The then Grand Secretary clearly recognised the need for Freemasonry to adapt and change. So have his successors. Nothing in the report suggested that our values or "distinctive character" needed to be amended. Our fundamental purpose and meaning, as expressed and communicated through our ritual, is not at risk.

However, the report also made it clear that we need to do a lot more to communicate who we are, what we do and how one becomes a member.

Implications for Lodges

The SIRC report gives us cause for optimism. Half of all men want to know more about Freemasonry and a quarter would consider joining. I find it interesting that 26% is very close to the 23% of people who give time to membership organisations every month.

The only way into membership is through Lodges. Somehow or other we have to connect with these men and introduce them to Freemasonry.

Lodges, and their members, can approach this by being visible in their communities, open about their membership and by sharing their experiences with friends and others in their working and personal networks.

However, doing so is not always easy. We know there are negative perceptions of Freemasonry in our society. What effect do these have and how do we combat them?

The C|T Group survey

In 2018 the then Grand Secretary, VW Bro. Dr. David Staples,[30] commissioned C|T Group[31] to survey attitudes towards Freemasonry. They found[32] that, in relation to organisations in general:

1 Organisations with a clearly defined purpose have a place in today's society.
2 Honesty and respect are the most frequently sought-after values.
3 Social and community aspects are the biggest draw to join a club.

4 Most were turned off from perceived secretive and religiously affiliated clubs.

However, when it came to Freemasonry:

1. 11% viewed Freemasonry favourably and 38% viewed it unfavourably.
2. 51% were either neutral towards Freemasonry or didn't have an opinion.
3. Reasons given for unfavourable views included secrecy (43%), undue influence / self-serving (23%), strange / rituals / shady / suspicious (12%) and elitist / exclusive (9%).
4. 7% of those who viewed Freemasonry unfavourably mentioned it being sexist or men-only.
5. 11% did not know why they viewed Freemasonry unfavourably.

When asked to describe Freemasonry:

1. 37% called it a secret society and 13% called it a cult.
2. 13% called it a private members' club, 5% a networking organisation, 4% a charitable organisation, 4% a fraternity, 3% a social club and 2% a religion.
3. 21% did not know how to describe Freemasonry.

When asked whether they would join:

1. 11% said they would.
2. 69% said they would not.
3. 20% did not know.

After being provided with some basic accurate information about Freemasonry, the 11% who viewed it favourably increased to 27% and the 38% who viewed it unfavourably reduced to 27%. Those who were neutral remained the same (39% rather than 38%) while the "Don't knows" reduced from 13% to 7%.

The survey identified elements of Freemasonry's language which contributed towards negative perceptions. C|T Group recommended that UGLE should:

1. Define the organisation in a way that clearly and concisely states who the Freemasons are and what they do and the role they play in the community.
2. Help potential members further understand what the Freemasons do by exemplifying typical activities, especially those that benefit the community, such as community outreach, monthly lodge meetings, dinner events or volunteering activities.
3. Contextualise. Demonstrate that the Freemasons provide a structure of support for their membership and the local community that combats the uncertainty and division in today's society.
4. Highlight the values that Freemasonry promotes – such as integrity, respect, friendship, compassion and support – and how they are just as relevant – indeed urgently needed – today as they ever have been.
5. Modernise. Use updated language to describe the Freemasons' values; be aware of the potentially negative impact of phrases such as "strict moral code" and "Supreme Being".
6. Emphasise the inclusive nature of the Freemasons, that the organisation is open to those of all backgrounds regardless of class or race.
7. Make it easier to find information about the Freemasons and the role they play in their local community.

In response, UGLE devised a "strategic narrative" to articulate Freemasonry more clearly and accurately, using everyday language. It has asked us all to use this narrative when communicating with the public. This will present a clear and consistent message and help "normalise Freemasonry within the public consciousness."

Implications for Lodges

It seems an increasing number of members accept that Freemasonry needs to be more visible and open. More and more Lodges are raising their profile within members' networks and their wider communities.

When planning any communication with the public, Lodges ought to adopt the language used by UGLE, so that together we can deliver a consistent message. This applies to face-to-face and written communication, and to traditional and digital channels.

UGLE's website contains clear statements about Freemasonry.[33] Its Frequently Asked Questions (FAQs)[34] provide members and visitors with answers to many questions. In addition, the Metropolitan / Provincial / District Communication Officers and their teams are available to help when framing words to use.

For individual members, the issue can be one of confidence. They may face initial disinterest or negative comments when they talk about Freemasonry. The survey shows that when Freemasonry is properly described negative attitudes can shift. We need to help members overcome their reticence.

The problem for many members is knowing how to describe Freemasonry. The language of the ritual does not help. In fact, reciting passages may well increase the impression that Freemasonry is a form of cult. Nor does it help to repeat tired phrases such as, "We are not a secret society. We are a society with secrets". This particular one only draws attention to secrecy. It creates confusion as the recipient struggles to make a distinction. It fuels negative perceptions and reinforces the idea that we have something to hide.

The key is to talk in everyday language. We can draw upon the words used in UGLE's resources. We can also speak from personal experience. We then come across as authentic, sincere and genuine. The Members' Pathway[35] offers guidance to help members to prepare their own "personal statement" about Freemasonry and how to talk about it with confidence and fluency.

If damaging myths and misconceptions about Freemasonry can be dispelled, and replaced with accurate information conveyed with conviction, perhaps some of those who say they won't join might eventually be attracted to the Craft.

Why is the bucket leaking?

The data from the above surveys and reports establish that:

1 Significant numbers of people still wish to join and contribute to community-based membership organisations.
2 Freemasonry is still relevant, if widely misunderstood.
3 If we can communicate our message more clearly many might be interested in joining.
4 We are actually very successful at introducing new members.

Yet, still we are in decline. Why?

The problem is not finding new members. The problem is, we are not keeping them. Before trying to find new members, perhaps we should address the problem of excessive resignations.

Let's fix the leaky bucket before we attempt to fill it. After all, there is no point in wasting good water!

The main source of data on member satisfaction within UGLE comes from the Membership Focus Group (MFG). The MFG was set up in 2014 by the then Pro Grand Master. It was chaired by RW Bro. Ray Reed, Past Provincial Grand Master for Buckinghamshire and the then Deputy President of the Board of General Purposes. The MFG found that 1 in 5 (20%) of all new members resign before being presented with their Grand Lodge certificate.

On behalf of the MFG, W Bro. John Roscoe, a Chartered Occupational Psychologist, conducted a survey to examine the issues.[36] He received 6,381 responses and found:

1 Although prepared well for Initiation, new Freemasons felt less well prepared for their next steps. 84% of Entered Apprentices believed that generally we met their needs. This fell to 69% for Master Masons and was 70% for Masters / Past Masters, 72% for Metropolitan / Provincial / District Grand Officers and 75% for Grand Officers.
2 There is a significant relationship (a correlation of 0.35) between the quality of care for new members and the change in membership numbers. Those Provinces which provided better

care were better at increasing (retaining) their membership.
3 The key factors that contributed to member satisfaction were, in order of importance:

   i   Feeling valued as a Member
   ii   Developing new friendships
   iii   Developing my masonic knowledge
   iv   Feeling included
   v   Social activities
   vi   Developing skills in ritual
   vii   The Lodge looks after its members
   viii It meets your social needs
   ix   There are natural leaders in the Lodge that support and motivate new members
   x   Attending Lodge of Instruction
   xi   Help in running the lodge or events
   xii   Being a member of the Royal Arch.

4 Over half of all members reported being very happy as a member. This increased with length of service from 55% for those who have been members for three years to 100% for those who have been members for more than forty-one years.
5 Seven percent of members were unhappy with their membership. A further 19% were neither happy nor unhappy (ie, neutral). 26% of all members reported being less than happy.
6 18.6% of new members (ie, less than 8 year's service) who were proposed by someone they already knew were happy or very happy with their membership. 49.1% of those who were self-referred (ie, approached us) felt the same.
7 If they remain members long enough (ie, for more than 8 years), this pattern reversed. 76.2% of those who joined through the traditional route were happy or very happy. 41.4% of self-referred members were happy or very happy. Feeling valued and feeling included accounted for the biggest difference between those who joined through the traditional versus the self-referred route.
8 The majority of members (73%) felt that the cost of Freemasonry

was about right. There was no significant difference due to age. Neither was location a major factor. 27% of those in London (where the cost is highest) reported dissatisfaction, the same as the average for all areas. However, those less involved were more dissatisfied with costs than those who were more involved.

9 Only 2.5% of those who were unhappy with their membership also reported that the cost of Freemasonry was too high. Feeling valued and included had a much bigger impact on members satisfaction than costs.

10 Most Freemasons (76%) were happy with the level of focus on charitable giving. However, 18% considered there is too much emphasis. Charitable giving did not feature in the top twelve factors that result in member satisfaction.

11 A number of members were concerned about the un-Masonic behaviour of senior members. These included unwelcome pressure, pomposity, patronage, nepotism and disrespect. Others suggested that the culture of many Lodges needed to change. They need to stop believing that "one size fits all." Instead they should appreciate and accommodate the diverse needs, interests and circumstances of new members.

Implications for Lodges

Twenty-six percent of members feeling less than happy is very high. Such members are at risk of submitting their resignation. The survey shows their dissatisfaction was not due to costs. Feeling valued and included was much more important than costs. Where good quality care is given and expectations are met, more members are retained.

The top twelve factors that contribute to member satisfaction are listed above. Feeling valued and feeling included explained the difference in satisfaction between those who joined through the traditional route and those who were self-referred. We seem to have paid a lot of attention to the latter group. Have we neglected the former? Are we assuming the proposer takes care of satisfying their candidate's needs? Is the proposer always a good personal mentor? Are they alone capable of making sure a new member feels valued and included by the whole Lodge? Are they alone responsible for developing their Masonic knowledge? Should Lodges be more proactive in understanding and meeting the needs and expectations of all their members?

If a Lodge is to grow, it must make sure there are no leaks in its bucket. It must attend to and resolve any issues that might prompt someone to leave. After all, a member is only likely to remain a member for as long as the Lodge, and Freemasonry itself, satisfies at least some of their needs or interests. They are even less likely to remain if there are any specific issues that cause dissatisfaction.

It should be a lot easier to keep existing members than it is to find new ones. An existing member has at least some commitment to the Lodge and its members. Their Lodge has at least some knowledge of them and what they want. To retain their membership the Lodge has to make sure their membership is more valuable and satisfying to them than the alternatives. Finding a new member is much harder.[37]

Every member who resigns is a lost member, a lost officer, and perhaps a lost friend, for every year of their life, not just the one in which they leave.

It is not true, as I often hear from Lodge Secretaries, that "we have no alternative but to accept this resignation". Rule 183 of UGLE's Book of Constitutions allows a Lodge to invite a member to withdraw their resignation.[38]

In addition, there are many warning signs or early indications that a member is dissatisfied and may be considering resignation. If action is taken early, we can often re-engage a member and prevent a resignation. Again, the Members' Pathway offers guidance in this area.

A good first step for a Lodge is to survey its members and share its analysis of the responses. Then it can debate what is working well and what could do with improving. The next step is to agree and implement a plan for the future. The Members' Pathway outlines how to do all of these actions and chapter 7 of this book looks at how a Lodge can manage change.

So, let's assume you have done this. You now understand why your Lodge's bucket is leaking and have taken steps to fix it. You can now consider how to attract more people into membership. Let us start with a consideration of why people join.

Why do people become Freemasons?

People join an organisation because it has some positive appeal to them. They think there is something interesting or good about it. Or that it will meet some need of theirs. Or it will offer them something that they think is of benefit. This could be a sense of feeling valued, satisfaction, enjoyment, friendships, a sense of purpose, opportunities to contribute or to achieve something worthwhile.

Before we did the ground-breaking work on adult recruitment in The Scouts, it was not uncommon to see notices in shop windows pleading for people to become a leader. "Otherwise the Cub Pack will have to close", they would typically read. Inevitably these cries for help failed dismally. They were not appealing and did not offer the potential volunteer anything positive. Why would anyone want to join anything that appeared desperate or was failing?

The precise motives for joining Freemasonry will vary from person to person. They will largely depend on each person's individual needs and circumstances.

In another study, this time for the Metropolitan Grand Lodge & Chapter of London, W Bro. John Roscoe examined why people join Freemasonry.[39] His research, based on interviews and a questionnaire, identified nine different motives or reasons:

i   History and Tradition
ii   Respect and Status
iii To be a "Better man"
iv   Pure curiosity
v   Mystic interest
vi   Escape!
vii Family connection
viii Because of a friend
ix   Sociable altruism.

John compared these with an academic model of values[40] and found a high degree of overlap. He concluded that people might find, "Freemasonry is a potential vehicle for expressing their underlying values and that this expresses something that is fundamental to them as people".

Implications for Lodges

If a new member finds that Freemasonry lives up to their hopes and expectations, they are likely to feel they made the right decision to join. They are likely to enjoy their membership and put more time and energy into it. However, if their reasons for joining are not satisfied, they will feel disappointed. They are less likely to remain a member for very much longer.

For a new member, the burden of satisfying their expectations of Freemasonry as a whole will fall mainly upon their Lodge. This is a big responsibility. If the Lodge has been careful to admit only those whose expectations it can meet, it may retain most of its new Initiates. However, if there is a mismatch between what the member wants and what the Lodge can offer, the Lodge is likely to lose that member.

This is why we built the creation of a Lodge outline into the Members' Pathway. A Lodge outline is the result of a Lodge's detailed consideration of what makes it distinctive and attractive, what is working well and what is not working well. We included a tool to help a Lodge review John's nine motives for joining and to build the results into its outline.

The reason members often give for resignation is a change in their circumstances. Normally more details only become clear if and when people outside of the Lodge get involved.[41] At this point the member often explains some level of dissatisfaction, together with a "tipping point" event. The dissatisfaction can normally be traced to a mismatch between what the member wants and expects and what the Lodge actually delivers.

Our bottom-up system of membership does not make it easy for a person who has "joined the wrong Lodge" to transfer to another. Except in Provinces which have put a scheme in place, once a member resigns form their Lodge there is no one supporting them. If they look for another Lodge, it would be on their own initiative. It then takes two meetings for an application to join another Lodge to be approved. Too often, the member just leaves Freemasonry.

Freemasonry as a whole is capable of satisfying all the nine different motives for joining. However, no one Lodge is likely to be able to meet them all. We need more diversity between Lodges, more "small variations" in Darwinian evolutionary terms. This will create more options for potential members. It would help if more Lodges referred "poor fit" applicants to Lodges better suited to their needs. Perhaps the Lodges that meet in the same Masonic Hall can discuss what features distinguish each of them from the others. They might identify opportunities to collaborate and support each other in some activities, and to specialise in others.

Light Blues Clubs complement what is available from Lodges. They play an important part in meeting wider expectations, especially if they offer more than social activities. However, they are not a substitute for good Lodge management.

If people join organisations for their positive appeal and a match with their own needs or interests, there is another implication for Lodges. As well as being clear about their distinctive features, Lodges also need members who are active, positive and enthusiastic advocates when talking with others. To understand why, we need to consider the next question.

How do people join Lodges, or any other membership organisation for that matter?

How do people become Freemasons?

Masonic convention says that we do not invite people to become Freemasons. They have to ask. North American Freemasonry expresses this as, "To be one, ask one" (2B1Ask1). The reason is, candidates and members are "seekers of light". Membership is not granted automatically to all applicants. It depends upon interview and a ballot. It cannot be promised by any existing member.

How does this fit with how people actually join membership organisations? Do they join on their own initiative? Do they volunteer or approach the organisation with a request to join? Or do they wait to be approached or invited?

According to the latest Cabinet Office report on volunteering and membership organisations, 71% of people join a membership organisation through word of mouth. 20% join through prior contact with the organisation. The remaining 9% approach the organisation as a direct result of a promotional activity, whether that be a leaflet, an event, website, or media activity.[42]

This data matches a 1992 report by Volunteer Centre UK, which showed that 91% of all "volunteers" only join an organisation after being approached by an existing member.[43] This finding prompted The Scout Association to develop a new way to recruit adult volunteers. I was a member of The Scouts' working group that developed its very successful "Six-step approach to adult recruitment" and was an author and the editor of its guidance materials.

The explanation for this finding is simple. Most people don't put themselves forward, even if interested. The reason seems to be, they don't want to be rejected. Rather than risk being turned away, many would much rather wait to be asked. They can then enjoy the pleasant glow of being wanted. Obviously, there are exceptions. 9% – but only 9% – approach the organisation themselves. For us, these are the people who enquire about Freemasonry via our websites, over social media and at our open events.

Yet many current members of both The Scouts (still!) and Freemasonry seem to assume that the way to "recruit" new members is to promote ourselves. They then assume the interested ones will approach us. There is no data to support these assumptions.

In recent years Freemasonry has become much more visible. We make extensive use of websites and social media. We wear regalia at public events. We organise open days and have a presence at community events. If such activities only introduce a few of those who might join a membership organisation, what is their purpose?

First, promotional activities do attract some enquirers who go on to become members. 9% join in this way. Secondly, in the words of the Members' Pathway, promotion and visibility create a "positive public image". An improved public image may prompt someone to be interested or curious. The C|T Group report demonstrates that accurate information can change attitudes. Thirdly, and perhaps most importantly, promotion increases our visibility and "normalises" us in the public perception. This makes it easier for our members to approach others and to start a conversation about Freemasonry.

Implications for Lodges

The data says that only a small minority of those who eventually join membership organisations put themselves forward. Most join as a result of a one-to-one conversation with an existing member or previous involvement with the organisation. That member approaches the "recruit". They either ask them to join, or they suggest that a request to join would be favourably received.

The Volunteer Centre UK's findings completely changed how we recruit new adult volunteers in The Scouts. No longer do local units expect the centre to find new leaders for them. The next generation of Scout Leaders are already within their local communities and networks. The Scouts just have to find them. We put together a package of resources and workshops, to help them define what and who they needed and to target the best people for the job. It led to The Scouts' largest ever increase in new leaders. Together with an improved youth programme, it facilitated major growth in the number of young people joining Scouting.

The Members' Pathway offers a parallel for Freemasonry. It was inspired by the approach we adopted in The Scouts. However, it was built around the culture, rules and processes within Freemasonry. At its heart is the same core principle that worked so well for The Scouts. If we want more members, we have to identify suitable people, approach them, discuss Freemasonry, answer their questions and guide them through the introductory stages of membership.

No Province, District or even Grand Lodge can do this for their Lodges. Every Lodge has to find its own potential members and reach out to them. The Members' Pathway document "Where new members come from" is designed to help Lodge members identify suitable people in their own networks. The documents "Promoting your Lodge" and "Explaining to others what Freemasonry means to you" helps them to approach those people, act as advocates for Freemasonry, talk appropriately about it and help them decide whether they wish to apply to join.

A perspective from the USA

All the above relates to Freemasonry under UGLE. However, is membership decline and its patterns unique to that jurisdiction? Can we learn anything from the country with the highest number of members?

In terms of numbers, membership of US Lodges peaked at over four million in 1959 and is now below one million.[44] Its decline matches that in UGLE.

The results of a 2016 survey of Freemasons across the USA, conducted by Jon T. Ruark, suggests that, if the current trend continues Freemasonry there will all but cease to exist by 2040.

Apparently, almost one in four members of US Lodges did not find what they were looking for when they joined Freemasonry. This is almost exactly the same as John Roscoe's finding that 26% of members of UGLE Lodges were less than happy with their membership. Further, for every new member joining Freemasonry in the USA, at least one chose to leave. As with UGLE, men in the USA still want to join Freemasonry. However, their Lodges have similar difficulty satisfying the expectations of new members and keeping them.

There were three key aspects of Freemasonry for which Ruark reported 90% agreement.

Against a background of rates of loneliness having doubled in the USA in the last fifty years[45], he found that 93% of American Freemasons appreciated the camaraderie of Freemasonry. Angel Millar has suggested that, "The fraternity has something to offer that most people desperately need and naturally want but cannot find elsewhere. Indeed, the lodge offers more than camaraderie. It is where we experience the bond of brotherhood that is stronger than most friendships."[46]

Ruark also found that nearly 90% of US Freemasons believed education about Freemasonry and its method of self-improvement was either important or very important. Yet 65% said that their Lodge provided such education only sometimes or never. In fact, he found that those who were least satisfied with Freemasonry were members of the Lodges that provided little or no education about it. As a result of the MFG's research, UGLE recognised this importance of education for a member's experience and so created the Solomon platform, to offer high quality online learning materials to all.

Finally, Ruark found that over 90% of US Freemasons reported themselves between moderately and very spiritual. In fact, only 13% were very active in religion while 37% considered themselves very spiritual. More widely in America, according to the Pew Research Center, those who consider themselves to be religious are in decline while those who consider themselves to be spiritual are growing in number. Increasingly, younger people are claiming to be spiritual but not religious.[47]

Implications for Lodges

The data from the USA is consistent with that which we have for Lodges under UGLE. However, Ruark's three "90% findings" deserve special consideration. Angel Millar suggests these should be our main focus.

The first is to position Freemasonry as a counterpoint for loneliness, by emphasising brotherhood. The second is to deliver better quality education about Freemasonry and explain more clearly its approach to self-improvement. The third is Freemasonry's capacity to satisfy a growing interest in spirituality without getting involved in religion.

Taken together, these three features comprise a unique offer. While some other organisations might offer one, I can think of no other organisation for adults that can satisfy all three.[48] Concentrating on them might help our Lodges attract suitable members, create greater membership experiences, and improve member satisfaction.

In conclusion

To summarise the above:

1. The membership of our Lodges has been in decline for around forty years.
2. The size of the decline (44.3% in the last 21 years) poses an existential threat if it continues for the next 20 years.
3. The decline is mainly due to resignations exceeding new members.
4. Each year around 8,000 people become Freemasons and around 11,000 resign from Lodges.
5. The number of Initiations is slowly reducing.
6. Thanks to strategies to improve retention, resignations are reducing more quickly than the reduction in Initiations.
7. At current rates it will take around 15 years for Initiations to exceed resignations.

8   To achieve growth sooner, Lodges need to reduce resignations using better preventive measures.
9   This means we have to be better at understanding and satisfying members' interests, needs and expectations.
10 We also need to become better at treating people as individuals, each with unique and diverse interests, needs and circumstances.
11 Freemasonry has the capacity to satisfy peoples' reasons for joining community organisations.
12. It also has a unique capacity to satisfy increasing needs for camaraderie – or brotherhood – and interests in learning, self-improvement, and spirituality.
13 Delivery is more difficult to achieve in a small or struggling Lodge.
14 More people might join if negative perceptions of Freemasonry were replaced with a modern description that positioned Freemasonry as relevant in the 21st century.
15 Most people join membership organisations as a result of being approached or because of previous contact.
16 Promotional activities directly generate only a minority of new members.
17 Promotional activities do increase awareness, create a "positive public image", stimulate interest and make it easier for us to talk about Freemasonry.
18 Lodges should not expect others to generate sufficient members for them to grow.

I firmly believe growth will only come when more Lodges satisfy members' expectations and provide a great membership experience. A Lodge can do this by first identifying and addressing its internal issues, to make itself "fit for the future". Then it can look externally to how it can find and introduce new ones. I call this strategy, "Inside – out".

The Members' Pathway and its tools and techniques offers Lodges the means to do exactly this.

We do not yet know the full impact Covid-19 will have on Freemasonry and its membership. Early indications are that the trend in a gradual reduction in resignations has not changed. However, there were fewer opportunities for Initiations during the pandemic. History tells us that crises also create opportunities for change. Lodges and Provinces that have reached out to their communities and networks are already seeing former members wish to return and potential members queue to join. Some Lodges used the time during the pandemic, while normal Masonic activities were restricted, to regroup and agree a new way forward. The Lodges that embrace these opportunities are likely to have a better future than those who do nothing.

In the next chapter, I look at Freemasonry from the candidate or member's perspective and from the context of their life and work.

---

[1] United Grand Lodge of England Annual Report 2021, p29.
[2] Total Initiations in the ten years to the end of 2019 was 86,802. Total resignations in the same period were 122,253. (Source: UGLE.)
[3] At 31/12/2019 UGLE had 188,401 individual members holding 239,435 individual memberships. (Source: UGLE.)
[4] Source: Paper of Business for the March 2022 Quarterly Communication of Grand Lodge, UGLE.
[5] Robert Putnam (2000), "Bowling Alone: the collapse and revival of American community", Simon & Schuster.
[6] John Lane (1895), "Masonic Records 1717-1894", 2nd Ed, Reprinted 2000, Lewis Masonic.
[7] "The Grand Lodge of All England, held at York" and "The Grand Lodge of England, south of the River Trent".
[8] John Lane (1889), "A Handy Book to the Lists of Lodges", London.
[9] Source: Paper of Business for the March 2022 Quarterly Communication of Grand Lodge, UGLE.
[10] P.R. James (1967), "The Union and after, 1813-1917", in "Grand Lodge 1717-1967", UGLE.
[11] Lodge No. 1593 was the last to be formed in 1875 and No. 2134 was the last in 1885.
[12] Lodge No. 3913 was the last to be formed in 1918 and No. 5095 was the last in 1928.
[13] Lodge No. 6222 was the last to be formed in 1945 and No. 7436 was the last in 1955.
[14] Since 1895 UGLE has published the number of Lodges on the Roll in the proceedings of Quarterly Communications.

[15] See the Book of Constitutions, rule 155.
[16] Source: Paper of Business for the March 2022 Quarterly Communication of Grand Lodge, UGLE.
[17] Based on 239,435 memberships at 31/12/2019 across the then 7,175 Lodges.
[18] UGLE closed up Lodge numbers twice during this period, in 1832 and in 1863.
[19] Charles Darwin (1859), "On the Origin of Species", John Murray.
[20] The Members' Pathway is at https://b.ugle.org.uk/membership/members-pathway.
[21] See https://www.gov.uk/government/statistics/community-life-survey-201920.
[22] The Office for National Statistics estimates that there were 23,229,412 males aged 18 and over in England & Wales in mid-2019 (see https://ons.gov.uk).
[23] See https://yougov.co.uk/topics/philosophy/trackers/brits-beliefs-about-gods.
[24] An estimated 1,391,256.
[25] Based on 186,240 members in England & Wales, the Isle of Man and the Channel Islands (source: Grand Secretary's presentation to the UGLE Membership Conference on 21st May 2019).
[26] See https://www.gov.uk/government/statistics/community-life-survey-2018-19. The equivalent has not yet been published for the 2019-20 survey.
[27] See http://www.sirc.org/about/about.html.
[28] See the UGLE press release 9th March 2012.
[29] Since 2014, RW Bro. Nigel Brown, PJGW.
[30] Since 2022, RW Bro. Dr. David Staples, PJGW
[31] See https://ctgroup.com.
[32] From the Grand Secretary's presentation to the UGLE Membership Conference on 21st May 2019.
[33] See https://www.ugle.org.uk/about-freemasonry.
[34] See https://www.ugle.org.uk/about-freemasonry/frequently-asked-questions.
[35] See https://b.ugle.org.uk/membership/members-pathway.
[36] John Roscoe (2015), "Results of the analysis of the second survey of Freemasons concerned with recruitment and involvement", report for the MFG.
[37] It is estimated that service organisations spend eight times as much effort to get one new customer than they do to serve and retain an existing one. See also Frederick F. Reichheld & W. Earl Sasser, Jr (1990), "Zero Defections: Quality Comes to Services", Harvard Business Review, Sept-Oct edition.
[38] If they then withdraw their resignation within 60-days it will be cancelled, and they will remain a member of the Lodge.
[39] John Roscoe (2015), "Results from a survey of new Initiates in London", presentation for MetGL / MetGC.
[40] See S.H. Schwartz (1992), "Universals in the content and structure of values:

Theory and empirical tests in 20 countries." In M. Zanna (Ed), "Advances in experimental social psychology (Vol. 25, pp. 1-65)." Academic Press, New York.

[41] For example, Metropolitan Grand Lodge & Chapter contacts resigning members soon after their resignation is received. They have been very successful at retrieving some members, albeit normally to new Lodges and Chapters.

[42] N. Low, S. Butt, P. Ellis and J. Davis Smith, (2007). "Helping out: a national survey of volunteering and charitable giving", London: Cabinet Office (conducted by the National Centre of Social Research and the Institute of Volunteering Research).

[43] Rodney Hedley (1992), "Volunteering Today: facts and figures on volunteering in the UK for volunteer organisers", Volunteer Centre UK.

[44] Source: Masonic Services Association of North America. See https://msana.com/services/u-s-membership-statistics/.

[45] Shainna Ali (2018), "What you need to know about the loneliness epidemic", Psychology Today.

[46] Angel Millar (2019), "The future of Freemasonry: who we are and what we have to offer", The Plumbline, Vol 26, No. 4, Scottish Rite Research Society.

[47] Michael Lipka & Claire Gecewicz (2017), "More Americans now say they're spiritual but not religious", Pew Research Center.

[48] Scouting offers young people a very effective approach to brotherhood, self-improvement, and spirituality. See my 2012 Prestonian Lecture, "Scouting & Freemasonry: two parallel organisations?", details of which are at https://prestonian2012.org.uk/the-2012-prestonian-lecture/.

Chapter 3

The World of the 21st Century Freemason

At the end of the 1980s I left the Medical Research Council and moved into management consultancy. I specialised at first in Training and Development, building on my academic and professional training in psychology and education. Over the years I developed expertise in leadership, performance management and organisational change and development. I now work as a leadership coach and a corporate facilitator. I help executives, boards and senior leadership teams plan and deliver strategic change.

In parallel to my professional career, I had a central involvement in developing how The Scouts in the UK recruit, train and manage their adult volunteers. Not surprisingly, I have taken a special interest in Freemasonry's membership issues.

I have worked with many organisations in the private, public and voluntary sector over thirty years. In that time, I have observed seismic changes in the workplace. The changes directly affect the lifestyle, behaviour and expectations of the people we hope will become Freemasons. The world of the 21st century, and the mindset of 21st century candidate for Freemasonry, is very different to that of the 20th.

In this chapter I examine some of the differences and their implications for our Lodges.

Lodges must become "fit for the future". If Lodges don't understand these differences, they will not succeed in attracting, introducing and retaining the 21st century Freemason. Without the 21st century Freemason they have no future.

However, nothing that follows suggests any need to make any changes to our fundamental purpose, values, meaning or to our ritual.

What has changed?

The major change has been the pace of change itself. Change is accelerating at an alarming rate. In business we look at social, technological, economic, political, legislative, and environmental change.[1] None of these have stood still in the last few years. Major events, such as the economic crisis of 2008 and the Covid-19 pandemic, turbo-charge this acceleration and create "paradigm shifts".[2] A paradigm shift occurs when the prevailing order or mindset rapidly and completely alters. Our Lodges must adjust, quickly, or fall behind and lose members.

Up until the early years of the 21st century, managers used to reassure employees unsettled by change. They said, "things will calm down soon". Now, we advise them to put on their running shoes and be ready for rapid change. We exhort them to be flexible. To our grandfathers, today's working environments would appear chaotic. We describe them as dynamic or responsive. The point is, we cannot fight change. We have to keep pace with it.

For many of our Lodge members, Freemasonry is a haven from the outside world. When our longest-serving older members joined, their Lodges did not appear to change much at all. At the time we did not engage with our communities or the media. We froze many of our practices and became an island. We detached ourselves from the wider world. We are now trying to catch up to where we should have been long ago. Those long-serving members may be very unsettled by our efforts. To help them adjust, we are explaining that Freemasonry has always evolved and must continue to do so.[3] We have launched a number of initiatives and programmes to support our priorities and objectives. The Members' Pathway offers Lodges a toolkit for change. It includes a nine-step change management process. However we develop our Lodges, it is important that we take new and long-serving members with us through the change.

Many members are familiar with change management from their experience of work. They might reasonably expect their Lodges to use similar disciplines. Their other work experiences also influence their perception of Freemasonry and their acceptance of the way we operate.

The world of work in the 21st century

In the last forty years there have been major shifts in the way employing organisations function, make decisions and communicate. Employers now have different expectations of employees, and vice versa. The fundamental change has been a move from a "command and control" approach to management. Instead, employees are expected to think, create, decide and act for themselves.

Command and control began in military organisations. It was adopted by the civil and colonial services and other organisations. Decisions were made at the top of an elaborate and structured hierarchy. They were then sent "down" to subordinates. Each level in the hierarchy had precisely defined limits of authority and responsibility. Employees were given instructions and were expected to obey.

In the current information age and knowledge economy, command and control organisations are almost obsolete.

Today we use instantaneous global communication systems to receive and access information on a rolling basis. 24-hour news channels, web-based commercial systems, video-conferencing and social media connect supply chains and social networks across time zones. Customers and suppliers expect rapid responses to questions and requirements. If a company doesn't meet those expectations, their business goes elsewhere.

Traditional command and control structures cannot keep up. Their "junior staff" are not allowed to make major decisions. Getting a decision from the centre is time consuming. Command and control organisations take too long to respond.

Large differences in wage rates between east and west have increased competition. A focus on quality (that is, compliance to specification) and customer satisfaction has driven process improvement and cost reduction. The only edge most UK organisations have comes from our intellectual rather than manual capabilities. Organisations have upskilled employees and invested in education and culture change.

Innovation and creativity are at a premium. So are the abilities to understand diverse customers, build relationships, forge partnerships and be proactive and responsive.

None of these are fostered or rewarded in top-down, command and control, organisations. Quite the opposite. Creativity is stifled when you fear the disapproval of your boss. Making a mistake or a poor decision result in sanctions rather than improved learning.

Implications for organisational culture

For an organisation to thrive today, it has to give authority to act to even its most junior staff. They are at the coal face. They have to satisfy customers, solve problems, take decisions and act on them. The buzz word for this is empowerment. I think of it simply as "permission".

Of course, the directors of an organisation still hold ultimate authority and accountability. However, they now operate through flatter, more fluid, organisational structures. They inspire employees by communicating clear goals, values and policies. These create a framework or boundary in which employees think and act for themselves.

Today's successful organisations respond to fast changing external pressures. They are "agile", adept at managing change. They don't rely on rules and procedures. They expect people to understand goals and take the initiative. They require flexibility and adaptiveness in employees. In turn, employees learn to accept change much more quickly. This works as long as managers have the appropriate skills, and as long as employees are kept up to date and have matters explained to them.

Customer satisfaction has been elevated to one of an organisation's top priorities, after profitability, solvency, safety and legal compliance. As a consequence, we all now understand the power we have as consumers. We expect service and satisfaction from our suppliers, both at work and personally. If we don't get these, we take our custom elsewhere.

These changes have transferred directly to the membership arena. Members now have a customer mindset. They expect to be served and satisfied by their member organisations. They expect to be heard, to have their opinions considered and to have a say in decisions. They expect organisations to move quickly to implement change. They expect everything be managed well. Enjoyment alone is rarely enough to secure continued involvement. Member satisfaction is critical to member loyalty.

Implications for working people

Today's employees are less likely to have served in the military. They are less deferential to senior staff than their parents would have been. Organisations are also less formal in their structures, titles and dress codes. Flatter organisational structures, with fewer layers of hierarchy, bring senior and junior employees closer together.

The skilled employee of a modern agile organisation knows they are valued and respected. Their knowledge and skills are at a premium. They are treated well and consulted. Each is recognized as a unique person, not just a job title or number.

Professional employees are motivated by a sense of purpose and achievement, rather than duty. They work to agreed goals and are accountable for what they deliver rather than what they do. They are recognised and rewarded on results rather than effort. They do not clock in or out but work whatever hours are needed to get the job done. They have a "go bag" ready packed and by the door, so that they can travel at short notice. They are used to working across time zones.

They want to know *why* they are asked to do something. They want to ask questions, challenge and get truthful answers. They are used to being listened to, to being accountable for and explaining their thinking and actions, and to receiving feedback.

Their loyalty to their employer lasts for as long as the employer appreciates their value and is loyal to them. Their commitment is not instant or automatic. It grows over time from repeated satisfaction, enjoyment, understanding and appreciation. It also depends on other calls on their time and their priorities.

If this employee has management responsibilities, they will probably have received training in management skills. Their own manager will also have been trained. Management is now a Chartered profession[4] and management skills add value to the organisation. They provide an excellent return on investment (ROI).

Management development programmes typically train people in planning, communication, leadership, teamwork, decision making, problem solving and change management. "Graduates" of such programmes know how to set goals, organise the activities of others, manage resources and deliver results. They use different communication channels to get a message across to a clearly defined audience. They know the value of consultation, feedback and active engagement. They recognise that leadership is about achieving agreed goals by inspiring others to follow. They adopt different leadership styles or approaches, depending on the situation and needs of those they are leading. They recognise the strengths of different individuals and can harness them for the shared good. They understand the value of coaching, personal development and succession planning.

As a direct result of what they learned, one cohort of twelve managers I trained created added income and savings of over a million pounds within six months of starting their management development programme. No investment in equipment could have made such a return, especially in such a short time. [5]

Anyone in work will have experienced a number of corporate initiatives. Some will have been successful and some not. Initiatives will probably have addressed corporate strategies, values and policies. They will have required employees to concentrate on customer satisfaction, quality, teamwork, innovation and change. Employees will have learned that successful people take responsibility and are goal orientated, flexible, proactive and accountable.

Organisations are less bureaucratic in the 21st century. Business meetings are less formal than those of forty years ago. Less time is taken up with traditional meeting procedures. The procedures that are followed are functional and necessary. They are completed in the minimum possible time, so that everyone's energy is given to the core purpose.

When important decisions are to be made, attendees will have received information in advance of a meeting. They will be expected to have studied them and come prepared. Time will not be spent speculating on matters that cannot be resolved at that meeting.

Today's employee tends to be worldly wise rather than naïve. They are familiar with corporate politics. They will see through the motives of those with personal agendas. They will have experienced disappointment when people, plans or programmes do not live up to expectations. They may have developed a protective veneer of cynicism. They are likely to value honesty, transparency, authenticity and integrity.

They will have learned the value of creativity. They will create and consider multiple ideas before filtering and evaluating them to arrive at a decision. They know that the first idea is rarely the best and that collective thinking generates a better range of options. They also know the most senior person does not have a monopoly on the best ideas.

They will be used to regular reviews of their performance and development. At these they will account for their actions and receive objective and carefully thought through feedback. They will discuss and agree with their manager clearly defined goals for the future and the support they require if they are to achieve them. These meetings will be open, two way and constructive. They will react strongly if others make decisions about them without their active involvement.

Just as the 21st century employee has adjusted, so have their family, friends, associates and membership organisations. If they have not, they will probably be challenged by our employee and may lose their allegiance.

Implications for everyday life

Outside of work, our 21st century Freemason's wider world is very different from their parents'.

Escalating house prices mean that they may still live with their parents, or in shared rented accommodation with strangers or friends, until their thirties. Their social circle is likely to be wider, with less defined boundaries. They are friends with people of different political views, races, religions, colours, creeds and sexualities. At best they are sceptical of traditional political and class structures. At worst they reject or dissociate from them. They are more socially mobile and – once they have sorted their housing – are probably economically independent.

They may feel strongly about global or local causes. They use social media as their primary communication channel, not email. They communicate concurrently with people around the world, of different cultures and belief systems.

If they are in a relationship, it may be with a partner of the same sex. Both they and their partner will probably be working. If they have their own family, both partners will take a full part in bringing up the children and in helping in the home. Their employers' expectations and pressures may compete, requiring careful negotiation and compromise. If they have moved from their hometown, they will not have the support structure of the extended family to help them with childcare. They may have multiple families, as a result of different partnerships. They could have complex childcare responsibilities.

The 21st century Freemason will be concerned with their mental as well as physical health. They are more likely than their parents' generation to be open about mental health difficulties. They may seek advice and assistance without fear of stigma.

They will expect to live longer than their parents and may delay major events in their life. They will not expect the public care system to provide for them. They will make provision to ensure their own future comfort.

They will have plenty of choices as to how to spend their free time. The growth in the range of leisure activities open to them creates a buyers' market. They may experiment with a number of interests before settling on those to which they commit themselves long term.

Having done so, they will not want their time wasted. The do not think "voluntary" necessarily means "amateur". Rather, they expect their membership organisations to be well run. They will expect events and meetings to be well organised and executed. They will want to be treated well, like a valued customer. They want their expectations understood and satisfied. Having been taught that they must be flexible, they will expect others to be so, including the organisations they join.

Implications for our Lodges

Freemasonry has much to offer the 21st century Freemason. It can be a haven in which they can pause, forget their worries, contemplate and find meaning. They can meet people from different backgrounds, with different views, who will become lasting friends. They can build new skills and grow in confidence. They can develop as a more rounded person with a sense of purpose and meaning. They will find stability in something that becomes an enduring and meaningful part of their life.

However, none of this will happen if their Lodge fails to meet the 21st century Initiate's expectations and they leave.

Our 21st century Freemason will have joined the Craft for one or more of the nine different reasons identified by W Bro. John Roscoe (see chapter 2).[6]

The reasons John identified are:

1. History and tradition (because of Freemasonry's long history, its traditions and continuity)
2. Respect and status (because Freemasons and Freemasonry have respect and status in society)
3. To be a "Better man" (because Freemasonry is concerned with values and principle and offers a means to become a better person)
4. Pure curiosity (because they would like to know what it entails)

5 Mystic interest (because Freemasonry is concerned with symbolism, philosophy, moral lessons and spirituality)
6 Escape! (because it offers an escape and a sanctuary from day-to-day pressures)
7 Family connection (because of family history and connections with Freemasonry, and the opportunity to continue a family tradition)
8 Because of a friend (because a friend suggested it would be interesting and satisfying)
9 Social altruism (because Freemasonry has a strong charitable and community ethic and offers the chance to be part of and to give time to something that has social worth).

It is important a Lodge understands why a particular person wants to become a Freemason. If they join a Lodge that does not align with or satisfy their particular reason for joining, they will be disappointed and dissatisfied. With their relative inexperience they may resign altogether, rather than finding a more suitable Lodge. Our bottom-up membership system does not make it easy for a member to transfer to another.

The culture of some of our more traditional Lodges is opposite to what the 21st century Freemason may have experienced elsewhere. Lodges in which power is wielded by a few are unlikely to engage today's employee or retain their membership. Autocratic officers who withhold information, impose their will on others, are intolerant of what they perceive to be a "lack of commitment", treat members as pawns, and who fail to discuss or explain issues and decisions are directly contributing to the decline in Lodge membership.

Because they understand the importance of corporate values, the 21st century Freemason will expect Lodge members to behave according to Freemasonry's values. As they understand the importance of true leadership, they will only respect senior members if they set an example to others. They will not accept the authority of autocrats or bullies, whatever badge they wear.

We want today's employees and professionals to join, commit to and remain in our Lodges. To achieve that, we will need to treat them as valued individuals with a unique set of interests, expertise and potential. Good quality Masonic mentoring does precisely this. It puts the member and their needs first. However, a superficial approach to mentoring will fail. Any attempt to "process" such a member according to some standardised approach to new members will be met with dissatisfaction, leading to disengagement, leading to resignation. Members are not goods on a conveyer belt.

Learning why someone wishes to become a Freemason, and what they expect from membership, starts before their interview.[7] If the Lodge cannot satisfy their particular reasons for joining, can it guide them to one that will?

Once they are a member, the Lodge can do much to satisfy the member's expectations and motives for joining. Planned personal mentoring – providing each member with the information, personal contact and support that they want – is key.[8] So is recognising that a member's needs, wishes and circumstances change over time. "Continued mentoring"[9] keeps track of these and provides support throughout a member's Masonic journey.

One of the major reasons given for early resignations is a lack of, or poor quality, Masonic education.[10] Lodges no longer have to rely on knowledgeable members for this. Solomon – UGLE's online learning platform – offers credible, high quality, education for Freemasons.[11] Provinces have skilled speakers able to deliver and manage engaging talks, demonstrations, dramas, quizzes and debates.

To engage the 21st century Freemason, Lodges first have to be willing to evolve. That means adapting their traditions and practices to reflect the needs and circumstances of a changing membership. It also means being more flexible. This involves listening to members, valuing their creative thinking, considering and implementing (at least some of) their new ideas.

A reason some give for not doing this is tradition. Lodges are rightly proud of their traditions, but these too must evolve. Holding on to every past tradition gives our predecessors more of a say in our future than current members. It turns Lodges into memorials and museums. Perhaps every generation could review and contribute to evolving Lodge traditions. Lodges that regularly review their practices and create development plans are better placed to meet the needs and expectations of current and likely future members.[12]

Changing personal circumstances often have short- and long-term impacts. If a member misses a meeting at short notice it may not be a sign of poor commitment. It may simply be a reflection of their working reality. To accommodate such circumstances, Lodges can arrange for other members to shadow working officers, ready to step in when needed. Plans for officer progression may be disrupted through no fault of a member when their career takes an unexpected turn. Succession plans may need regular review.

Lodge meetings need to be attractive and enjoyable. They have to provide something much better than the alternatives open to members and visitors. Meetings and Festive Boards have to be planned, well organised and efficiently run. Time ought to be devoted to Freemasonry's important features and not wasted on drawn out administration. Meeting times ought to reflect its members' lifestyles and wishes. A Lodge can offer options to accommodate individual differences. For example, some offer a second entry after all administrative business has been conducted. Others offer early departure. Given the presentation quality of entertainment and education we now experience, ritual and ceremonial needs to be of a high standard and meaningful. The 21st century Freemason is used to quality and expects it in his social as well as his working life.

Lodge officers today are called upon to demonstrate good management practices. They are expected to communicate well, consult, adopt different leadership styles (according to the needs of people and situations) and involve all members in the running of the Lodge.

The more successful officers build individual relationships with new members. They find new ways to involve members, according to their talents and wishes. They reach agreements that are reviewed and updated at intervals. They discuss and explain issues, not "tell them how it is". They recognise that the new member's membership costs the same as everyone else's. They treat every member as they would a valued customer. They recognise a member's Masonic development and involvement needs nurturing. They do not take others' membership, involvement and commitment for granted. They seek to be a role model who lives and exemplifies Masonic values.

Less successful officers treat new members like faceless squaddies, the next on a production line in an outdated – if it ever was appropriate – "one size fits all" form of Freemasonry.

If our Lodges are to survive, autocratic officers – even the most kindly and benevolent – will have to make way for those who can show leadership, recognise strengths, explain themselves and win the hearts and minds of their members.

Covid-19

At the time of writing, we are still learning to cope with the Covid-19 pandemic. In the UK, Lodges are meeting but some members still feel it is too early for them to return. It is certainly too early to evaluate the impact of the pandemic on our membership, although we can expect it to be significant. It is also likely to affect the mindset of the people we wish to attract.

Post Covid-19, the 21st century "potential candidate" will probably re-evaluate their priorities and their use of time. They may have even greater expectations of their organisations and less tolerance for inefficiency or bureaucracy. If there is a shift in priorities away from the material towards the meaningful, the world may become more caring and appreciative. However, if people feel threatened or a sense of loss, they may become more selfish.

Covid-19 is clearly a threat to Freemasonry and our Lodges. However, coming out of it there will also be opportunities. We need to be alert to new possibilities, open to change and ready to adapt to whatever the "new normal" offers or imposes.

Conclusions

Thanks to sustained efforts by UGLE and many of our Provinces and Lodges, Freemasonry is becoming more visible, recognised and respected. To use the last Grand Secretary's term, it is becoming normalised in the public's mind. Therefore, we now have the best opportunity for years to attract and introduce outstanding new members who will lead us into the future and ensure the continuance of our Lodges.

However, unless Lodges make adjustments in their practices and cultures, unless they evolve to become better aligned to 21st century lifestyles and mindsets, they may find they will not retain enough of these outstanding people to ensure the continued existence of Freemasonry as we know it.

If we don't make changes to our Lodge practices, the 21st century Freemason will do so – when their time inevitably comes.

We may as well start now.

In the next chapter, I consider change in the context of Freemasonry and why it is essential that Lodges modernise their management now, if they have not already done so.

---

[1] These stand for PESTLE and give their name to an organisational development technique called environmental appraisal.

[2] First described by Thomas S. Kuhn (1962), "The structure of scientific revolutions", University of Chicago Press.

[3] See, for example, FMT articles, the Pro Grand Master's addresses to Quarterly Communications of Grand Lodge and my 2018 Cornwallis Lecture, "The future of Freemasonry: evolution and change".

[4] The Chartered Management Institute (CMI) awards Chartered Manager (CMgr) status under the authority of its Royal Charter. See https://www.managers.org.uk. The author is a Fellow of the CMI (FCMI).

[5] As Benjamin Franklin said, "An investment in knowledge pays the best interest."

[6] You can find more information on John Roscoe's research into motives for becoming a Freemason in the Members' Pathway (see b.UGLE.org.uk/membership/members-pathway).

[7] The Members' Pathway describes in the Attract section how this can be achieved during the screening process before the interview (b.UGLE.org.uk/membership/members-pathway).

[8] Planned personal mentoring is described in the Engage section in the Members' Pathway (b.UGLE.org.uk/membership/members-pathway).

[9] Continued mentoring is also described in the Engage section of Members' Pathway (b.UGLE.org.uk/membership/members-pathway).

[10] See Chapter 2.

[11] See https://solomon.ugle.org.uk.

[12] The Members' Pathway provides tools for a Lodge review and planning process. See the Plan section (b.UGLE.org.uk/membership/members-pathway).

Chapter 4

We have NOT always Done it this Way

One of the many lessons I have learned working with so many organisations during my career is the need for all organisations to refresh themselves, to continuously evolve. No organisation, whether in the private, public, charity or not-for-profit / voluntary sector, can stand still while the outside world changes. To do so would lead to a disconnect with its customers, citizens, beneficiaries or members. They would then take their custom or loyalties elsewhere, to a provider that can understand and satisfy their needs.

Freemasonry and our Lodges are no different.

Nevertheless, when I first became a Freemason in 1991, I was told that things don't change much in Freemasonry. When I asked why we did something the way we did I was often told, "It's because we have always done it this way."

Based on my experiences since, I have to disagree. We have not always done Freemasonry this way. Looking back over Freemasonry's history for the last three hundred years, I know that Freemasonry has been constantly evolving, just like every other successful organisation.

In this chapter I will demonstrate this truth. Indeed, I believe we have survived until now, and often thrived, precisely because we have evolved. I will make the case for Freemasonry to continue to evolve and change. I will justify that by reference to the nature of evolution itself, historic precedent and by the need to reconnect with our communities and be relevant if we are to attract new members. I am going to draw on my experiences as a change manager and my work with other changing and successful organisations, including The Scout Association. I will suggest ways in which Lodges can manage a change process that will help to ensure their future.

In July 2021 United Grand Lodge published its new vision for the future. That vision is:

> To attract those from all backgrounds and walks of life, enabling them to develop into more thoughtful and confident people. To inspire and challenge them to practise the core values we celebrate – Integrity, Friendship, Respect, Charity – in their private and public lives. To cement our reputation as a force for good in our communities and society at large and as a thriving organisation that people aspire to join.

It went on to define its mission as:

> Over the next 7 years, we will enhance our reputation as a thriving organisation that people aspire to join and broaden our membership across all age groups.

The background to this work is a decline in membership over more than forty years, resulting in an organisation that is less than half the size of that in the 1960s. However, its infrastructure is a result of the expansion it had been through to accommodate the unprecedented post war growth.

Our membership has reduced to around what it was in 1920, under 200,000. However, we now have more than twice as many Lodges, many more Masonic Halls and a more complex organisation.[1] We are left with more Lodges than our membership can sustain and many of them are becoming weaker. With an average membership of 33.4, many Lodges don't have sufficient diversity of skills and interests to find motivated and enthusiastic people to fill the range of offices. Many find it difficult to plan a succession of officers, resulting in some remaining in office longer than they would like. This can lead to a loss of enthusiasm and energy, creeping complacency and eventually apathy.

If we put this situation in business terms, the market is flooded with supply, but demand has shrunk. Just as in business, the danger is that the suppliers, in this case our Lodges, will reduce quality to compete for customers, in this case new members.

This is what has happened. Some of our Lodges have stagnated and are not offering the experience that new and existing members want. Others appear to have lowered the bar for admission to bring in more members. I have even heard some brethren suggest we should abandon the requirement for a belief in a Supreme Being, simply to make it easier for applicants to qualify.

Despite the overall fall in membership some Lodges are thriving and growing. Freemasonry is proving very popular among young people, especially where it has the means to become a regular part of their social lives. Young members' groups are particularly successful in this respect. UGLE researched the difference between struggling and thriving Lodges and we used the findings when we developed the Members' Pathway.

This fall in membership has affected our attitudes. There is a widespread view that Freemasonry as an organisation is in difficulty. However, when we last had around 200,000 members, in the 1920s, we were then recognised and respected by the public and we were perceived as successful. We certainly were seen as a thriving organisation that people aspired to join in 1920.

Perhaps today we are comparing ourselves too much with the boom years of the 1960s. That is natural. It is within living memory.

However, if we do not develop a sense of optimism, we will not make the changes needed if we are to be recognised, respected and attractive once again. After all, nothing positive can come from negative thinking. Perhaps we should consider the post-war rise in membership as having the effect of a tidal wave. It created a temporary increase, and it did not shift our underlying numbers.

Should we accept that reality, adjust our expectations and seek to stabilise membership at between 200,000 to 250,000? We could then plan the use of our resources and create an infrastructure to support that level of membership.

However, what our Lodges have been doing for the last forty years has not arrested the decline, which has been at a steady rate. We cannot let this continue. So, our Lodges must do something different. We must change.

Change is the normal and natural state of all living things. Charles Darwin observed that all populations change over time. His theory of natural selection explains why some groups within populations thrive while others fail. Essentially, small variations between those groups result in some of them being favoured over others in the struggle for limited resources. Darwin himself said there is, "One general law, leading to the advancement of all organic beings, namely: multiply, vary, let the strongest live and the weakest die." Perhaps a more familiar quote is by Megginson who said, "It is not the strongest that survive, nor the fittest, but those best suited to their environment and best able to manage change". Carl Sagan said, "Extinction is the rule. Survival is the exception."

If we apply these points to Freemasonry, then we should realise that Freemasonry is just one organisation a person might choose to join. Equally, they have plenty of Lodges to choose from. Each Lodge must make its offer attractive to potential applicants. Each Lodge must introduce small variations to make itself distinctive in the hope that it will be favoured. Evolution also tells us that we cannot expect all our Lodges to survive; only those that are willing and able to adapt to their changing environments.

Currently around 2.24 million men in our country regularly give time to clubs, societies and organisations related to hobbies, social activities and recreation.[2] Do we have a fair share of this market? Are we becoming more attractive or less? Have we introduced small variations that are favourable to those making a choice of which organisation to join? Are all of our Lodges well suited to their environments and able to manage change?

Or, are we resisting evolution in our quest to maintain those traditions and practices that favoured the lifestyles of our forebears, but which are no longer relevant to today's Freemason?

If we resist evolution, we will die. Our Lodges must be willing to make those small variations over time, in the hope that some at least will be relevant and will find favour with today and tomorrows' applicants and members.

In 2016 I watched a TV programme in which the popular entertainers Ant and Dec (Anthony McPartlin and Declan Donnelly) followed the then Prince of Wales for a year and observed his work with the Prince's Trust. His Royal Highness, now King Charles III, had formed the Trust in 1976, shortly after leaving the Navy. In the following forty years it had grown to become a highly respected organisation, offering young people from difficult backgrounds the opportunity to make a good life for themselves. In one interview, either Ant or Dec (I never know which is which unless they are standing side by side) asked His Royal Highness about the future for the Trust. He replied that it would be wrong to continue doing things that were right a few years ago, just because they worked then. "The Trust", he said, "must evolve if it is to survive, it must adapt to continue to be attractive and relevant."

Incidentally, if you do not know who Ant and Dec are, they are two of our most popular entertainers today. They were born in the same year the Prince's Trust was founded, have been on our TV screens since the late 1980s and are much loved by the public at large. They seem to me to have their fingers on the pulse of our country today. They represent the sort of people we might wish to attract to Freemasonry. However, if we don't have some understanding of the world as experienced by those in their early forties today, we may well struggle to attract Ant and Decs' generation to Freemasonry.

As I explained in Chapter 3, the world in which the working Freemason lives is very different from that of 40 years ago. The nature of those changes is such that a smaller proportion of the population is likely to be available for Freemasonry. Certainly, fewer might perceive it to be for them – unless we become more visible and better recognised.

The growth in the range of leisure activities and opportunities then mean that we must compete with some very attractive pursuits if we are to bring good people into the Craft. Remember, evolution tells us that it is those best suited to their environment and best able to manage change that survive in competitive circumstances. Our Lodges must rise to this challenge.

What then has changed in the Craft in the last forty years and, indeed, in the last hundred years? I have already explained the tidal wave effect of increased members following the two world wars and how, over the last forty years or more, our numbers have returned to around what they were in 1920.

Internally there have been changes in our rules, procedures, structure and communication. Our Book of Constitutions has evolved to accommodate the law, external regulations and technology. Therefore, many of the procedures we are asked to follow have had to change, requiring Lodge officers to have new skills. New Lodge offices have also been introduced; first Charity Steward, more recently Lodge Mentor and then Lodge Membership Officer. In 2003 the Metropolitan Grand Lodge of London was formed, bringing the Lodges within five miles of Freemasons' Hall under its jurisdiction.[3] After many years of maintaining a distance from the press, UGLE is now promoting itself to the media and the public. Freemasonry now communicates directly with its members, using email and other digital technologies.

Looking at Freemasonry from the outside, we have also seen a change in the public's perception of us. In 1920 Freemasonry regularly appeared in the local and national press and we were seen in vary favourable terms. The Pro Grand Master at the time, The Earl of Ampthill, was regularly seen in Masonic dress at public events. The President of the Board of General Purposes, Sir Alfred Robbins, a journalist himself, ensured we had a very positive relationship with the media. Freemasonry was visible, recognised and respected, just as we wish it to be now.

In the 1930s we went underground. With the rise of fascism in Europe, and its threat to Freemasonry, we hid. Unfortunately, we did not come back into the light again until very recently. For many years we avoided contact with the "uninitiated and popular world". We stayed silent when criticised. Our silence created a perception that we had something to hide. As suspicion grew, we lost respect.

The more you read of Freemasonry's history the more you realise that the Craft has always evolved with the times. Grand Lodge and its constituent Lodges have had to adapt in response to outside and inside influences.

I will outline just two examples. In 1799 an unintended consequence of the proposed Unlawful Societies Act threatened to outlaw Freemasonry. Representatives of the two English Grand Lodges and the Grand Lodge of Scotland met with the Prime Minister, William Pitt, who was not a Freemason. They agreed changes to the Bill to exempt Freemasonry from its scope. However, they had to concede measures to ensure Freemasonry would not be hijacked by the seditious influences that the bill sought to restrict. Some of these measures survived until the 1967 Criminal Justice Act. More recently, following the Equality Act 2010, UGLE has introduced other adaptations to ensure that Freemasonry continues to comply with the law.

You will find further examples in your Lodge minutes, or the articles in *"Freemasonry Today"* by VW Bro. John Hamill. In the latter, John explains how things we might assume have always been done in a certain way have actually evolved and developed over Freemasonry's history, often in response to outside influences.

I have visited two of the three surviving Time Immemorial Lodges that together formed the first Grand Lodge in 1717. They do not keep to the practices they adopted then. While retaining some of their traditions, they have adapted and evolved over time. Today they are very efficiently run Lodges providing very meaningful Freemasonry to their members. Many other Lodges that arose in the 18th century, and indeed many other fraternal organisations, have long since died because they did not evolve.

Today many Lodges have resisted the call to evolve and seem unwilling to change. Their approach might have been relevant to candidates from forty years ago but that will not attract or retain today's man. These Lodges are like the ostrich that puts its head in the sand to avoid reality. However, Freemasonry as a whole cannot do that. Collectively we have to face the facts. If we refuse to do so we may deprive future generations of the opportunity to belong to a particular Lodge, or even to Freemasonry at all.

Perhaps one reason such Lodges have resisted evolution and change is that, when we hid from the public eye, we lost our ability to sense the impact of wider change and to develop incremental responses. It is as if we became an island detached from the wider world. We froze many of our practises and traditions and perpetuated them unaltered. We then began to believe that, "We have always done it this way" when history tells us that this is never true.

One reason often given for resisting change is a respect for tradition. Personally, I love tradition and enjoy many of the traditions associated with our country and its institutions. In fact, my love for tradition has been one of the reasons I have joined some organisations.

Equally, I believe tradition is a wonderful servant but a very poor master. G.K. Chesterton called tradition, "the democracy of the dead".[4] In other words, if we allow tradition to determine our future, we are giving our predecessors a bigger say in our affairs than our current members. Our predecessors made changes themselves, which they based on the situation in their time. However, they could not have anticipated the issues our members face today. Their decisions then could not be expected to satisfy our needs today and they cannot have been expected to future proof the Lodge.

It seems to me far better to allow tradition to evolve. One way is for each generation to make its own contribution to tradition. Past traditions can be reviewed. If they still serve your purpose and contribute to your success, then keep them. If they stand in the way of your future health and strength, they can be adapted or removed. This approach has served many of our long-standing institutions very well indeed, including the Monarchy, the City of London and our older Universities. In fact, allowing traditions to evolve is precisely what happens in our most successful older Lodges.

Today, I believe we have to reconnect with the world, become sensitive to wider social influences and evolve our organisation so that the way we operate is relevant and attractive. We can change many things without losing our purpose and meaning, and without altering our ritual. If we don't evolve and change, as natural selection tells us, we will die. Just as so many other Lodges and fraternal organisations did in the 18th and 19th centuries.

I have made the case for the Craft to evolve and change. I have justified that by reference to natural selection, historic precedent and by the need to be relevant if we are to attract new members. The question is, how do we change?

Nationally, the Scout Movement offers us a template. In that organisation, when we were considering major changes at the end of the 1990s, we spent considerable time consulting our members and listening to what they told us. Then we fed back to them the results. With its online surveys and with local and national discussion forums, UGLE is doing the same. Scouting concluded that its core values should not be altered. UGLE has done the same. No one is suggesting any change to our ritual, it's meaning or to the nature of the Masonic experience. UGLE does suggest, however, we use everyday language when talking about Freemasonry with those who are not members. Scouting also concluded that the way the organisation operated, recruited, trained and communicated with its members and with the public needed to be radically updated. We are currently going through a very similar process in Freemasonry.

For example, the Members' Pathway offers tools and techniques, adopted by thriving Lodges, for use by all of us. We now communicate direct to all our members who register for our websites and we are making extensive use of social media, which is the primary communication method used by people under fifty years of age. We will soon see changes in our Book of Constitutions. Solomon, UGLE's online learning platform, now offers everyone the chance to learn about their Masonic interests at their own pace. Hermes, an administrative front end to our membership system, will enable Lodge Secretaries to file updates and returns online. Our four central charities have consolidated into one organisation. This was partly to simplify operations, to become more efficient and effective at applying their resources. It was also to be better recognised and to have a bigger impact within the charity sector.

Freemasonry in England and Wales is going through its most extensive change in at least 100 years.

Provinces and Districts are responding to, and in many cases leading, these changes and developments. When new initiatives are set up, Freemasons drawn from around the country are recruited to their working groups. National conferences are held for Provincial and District Secretaries, Almoners, Charity Stewards, Mentors and Membership Officers, and Communication Officers. The Provincial and District Grand Masters and Grand Superintendents are consulted on major developments and approve them before they are launched. Pilot studies are run that include Provinces and Lodges from across our constitution.

How then can we manage change at Lodge level? Those who have studied the management of change agree that successful change, resulting in something that engages everyone and thrives, requires careful planning, consultation, the involvement of many, and regular communication with all. In Freemasonry we have the added requirement to maintain harmony in our Lodges. I offer you a process that you can choose to follow that can deliver all these results – if done well. This is in a series of nine steps.

1. Create an open forum for discussion about the future of your Lodge and include all members, not just the Past Masters. This is to gather all opinions, insights and ideas and not just those of your more senior members. The newer members have a stake in the future of your Lodge and need to be heard and involved in considering its future. Their ideas and contributions may lack an understanding of Freemasonry's conventions but equally they may be fresh and stimulating. Such a forum is quite different from the formalities of a Lodge committee.

2. Ask all members to consider and identify your Lodge's strengths and weaknesses, as well as the potential opportunities and the threats that it faces. Give members some time to think this over, perhaps by issuing a questionnaire in advance of any meeting. Accept and consider all opinions. At this point you are seeking to capture and acknowledge the range of views, not reach agreement or disagreement.

3 Ask every member to list (1) what they like about the Lodge and what they wish to see continue, (2) what they don't like about the Lodge and what they wish to stop and (3) what they would like to see introduced. Think of these in turn as Green, Red and Amber actions.
4 Compile these opinions and actions together and discuss them in the open forum. Try to agree a way forward on the basis of consensus. Consensus take time to achieve and normally means people have to compromise. It is not about <u>anyone</u> getting what they want. It is about <u>everyone</u> agreeing on something that they can all support. In matters such as the future of a Lodge it is better than voting because in voting some members will be unhappy with the result and may not support or work towards its implementation. With consensus all members become committed. This agreed way forward then forms your Lodge's agenda for change.
5 Identify whether there are any special features about your Lodge that represent variations from other Lodges, and which might help to promote the Lodge to potential members and visitors. Special or distinctive features make the Lodge attractive to certain people. For example, daytime Lodges attract people who cannot attend in the evenings and affinity Lodges attract people who follow a particular shared interest.
6 Agree a shared vision of what you would like your Lodge to be like in five to ten years' time. This might include from where the Lodge draws its members, the atmosphere in the Lodge, distinctive practices in the temple and at the festive board, how it operates, numbers and special interests.
7 Agree a plan of action and specific steps that, over a period of time, will gradually change your Lodge to be closer to your vision and which address your agenda for change. Include time scales for the plan, moving at a pace that is acceptable to the Lodge. Make it clear in the plan who is to do what, by when.
8 Meet regularly, as a discussion forum, to review the plan and its progress, to check that the changes are working and that members are informed and engaged. Modify the plan if necessary. Try to involve many different members in delivering the plan.

9 Celebrate your successes as they occur and make sure that others outside your Lodge and inside are aware. It can help to keep a record of the changes and successes, which will remind people of the "distance you have travelled" and will form a valuable part of the Lodge's history.

Just as change for the sake of change is foolish, so is remaining static for the sake of remaining static, as if preserving practices that are no longer relevant could ever sustain us in the future. If tradition is the "democracy of the dead", then as guardians and stewards of our Lodges, we have a duty of care to cast our vote to ensure their future.

We live in a crucial time in Freemasonry. Many Lodges are showing that it is possible to change the way that they work while retaining our purpose, values and the special nature of the Masonic experience. Grand Lodge is asking us to evolve and change. It is now up to us to do so.

The alternative is not something I wish to contemplate.

In chapter 7, I explain why some people resist change and offer some approaches to address resistance. Before then I want to consider leadership and management (chapter 5) and decision making (chapter 6).

---

[1] See Chapter 2.
[2] Op cit.
[3] See the Book of Constitutions, Rule 128.
[4] G.K. Chesterton (1908), "Orthodoxy", John Lane, The Bodley Head, London.

Chapter 5

Leadership and Management in the Lodge

Much of my professional career has been spent developing the leadership and management skills of people in diverse organisations, including the voluntary as well as private and public sectors. This has given me a fantastic insight into leaders and their approach to leadership and management.

As well designing and delivering bespoke leadership and management development programmes, I work as a leadership coach to senior employees. I have also been a trainer for The Scout Association for the last thirty years and have specialised in developing and delivering leadership training for its volunteers. My work has won industry awards and has been accredited by professional organisations.[1]

My own research into leadership and management has highlighted the need for both functions in all organisations, and for both to work together and complement each other. In fact, this is one of the basic tenets behind my own model of leadership and change, the Success Cycle.[2] I developed this model to align leadership and management, future vision and current action, so that all our energies and resources can be devoted to our long-term purpose. When an organisation is lacking in one or both of leadership and management, or in one or both of vision and action, then that organisation encounters problems.

These principles apply just as much to Lodges as they do to any other organisation, or units within organisations. In fact, the structure of our Lodges is ideally suited to balancing leadership and management, providing the relevant office holders understand the difference and have appropriate support from others.

I really ought to define what I mean by leadership and what I mean by management.

Many before me have sought to define leadership. I simply think of leaders as those who others choose to follow. Leadership is about providing purpose and direction for others and their activities. Leadership is idealistic and inspirational. It is concerned with the big picture, goals and aspirations. Leaders are recognised by others, rather than appointed by more senior people in the organisation. They are chosen because of their qualities more than their skills. Therefore, it is possible to have leaders who hold no position of authority other than the respect and support of their followers. When this happens, those who hold formal authority are often challenged.

Management is different, but complementary. It provides the organisation and disciplines necessary for our purpose to be fulfilled. It is practical, mechanical, detailed. It is concerned with plans, actions, and systems. Managers are appointed by more senior people in the organisation, often as a result of their skills and abilities – although I wish more account was taken of their values, attitudes and qualities. Skills can be learned, although all too many people find themselves in management positions before learning the skills, disciplines and techniques needed to be successful.

Of course, the above is a simplification. Leadership and management are not polar opposites. Many people act as both leaders and managers. What is important is that people who are meant to be leaders provide mostly leadership and perhaps some management and people who are meant to be managers provide mostly management and perhaps some leadership. Difficulties arise when a manager or leader underperforms in their primary role or overperforms in their secondary role.

Let's now apply this thinking to Lodges.

The Master is clearly expected to be a leader. By electing a Master every year, we create an opportunity for every member who satisfies the Lodge's criteria to provide the Lodge with a sense of purpose and direction. Annual election also means that we do not have to endure a poor Master for too long!

A Master who is a good leader – that is, one who provides purpose and direction and who others choose to follow – tends to leave the Lodge in a better condition than it was before them. Equally, the Master who becomes too heavily involved in the day-to-day management of the Lodge can create more problems than they solve. If there are already able and willing managers in post, their involvement is unnecessary. If there are not, their involvement can distract them from their primary role. The wise Master appoints able and willing people to the management roles and lets them do their job. Of course, if there are no able and willing people to take on the roles this becomes difficult. I will deal with this elsewhere.

So, who are the managers in the Lodge?

There are a number of them, and each are responsible for a different key area of the Lodge's activities.

The first is the Secretary. Technically and traditionally, they are the

Lodge's "Company Secretary", responsible for the administrative activities in the Lodge. They have to summon and record all meetings. They also have to ensure the Lodge in its functioning, including its formal business and decisions, complies with the Book of Constitutions and Provincial and Lodge by-laws, by advising the Master and others on these matters and by completing all the paperwork required by Masonic authorities.

These administrative activities are important, but they are not the reason we meet. Therefore, they should not take up the bulk of our meetings. They can be undertaken in a slick and efficient manner, to occupy minimal Lodge time and to help keep the focus on the core of Freemasonry, which centres around our ritual and our ceremonies. To streamline our meetings and minimise the time consumed by administration, the Lodge Secretary needs to make good use of technology and prepare everything in advance, in collaboration with others.

In practice, in many Lodges the Secretary tends to be more of a managing director than an administrator. They are often the driving force in the Lodge. By this I mean they are often the one who thinks ahead, ensures the Lodge has a plan for an active programme, communicates with the membership, encourages them to participate and provides sustainable drive and energy. If the Secretary is not the driving force, someone else – probably a Past Master – will need to be.

Lodge Secretaries clearly need to be well organised, detail conscious, good administrators and able to set up and run systems. Nowadays they have to be more than computer literate. They need skills in the use of office and web applications. They also need to be good communicators and be blessed with energy, tact, diplomacy and be trustworthy so that they can deal with confidential information.

The Secretarial team includes the Assistant Secretary, Treasurer, Charity Steward and Membership Officer as well as any members co-opted to assist them in their work. These might include brethren who run the Lodges social media or organise social events, for example. Although these are each responsible to the Master – and ultimately the Lodge – for the proper performance of their duties, they do need to work in collaboration with the Lodge Secretary to be effective in their roles.

The second manager is the Director of Ceremonies. They are

responsible for planning and directing all ceremonial and normally set the standard of ritual work.

Once again, they need to be well organised and able to plan ahead, based upon the annual plan agreed with the Master and the other managers in the Lodge. They can then select brethren to deliver ritual, giving them plenty of time to prepare. A Director of Ceremonies needs to have the respect of the members and an air of authority, to ensure ceremonial work is conducted with dignity, without being overbearing or dictatorial. They need to build good relationships with all members and work with others, such as the Lodge Mentor, to involve brethren in ceremonial and ritual work at a level appropriate to them.

The ceremonial team includes the Assistant Director of Ceremonies, the Chaplain, Tyler and all the progressive officers.

We then come to the care team. The manager of this team may vary from Lodge to Lodge, but it is likely to be either the Lodge Almoner or Lodge Mentor. What they have in common is a focus on the individual needs of each member, whether they be for health, wellbeing or Masonic understanding and education. These officers can share their understanding of members' needs, in confidence if need be, and co-ordinate their activities so that each member receives the care and support they require.

One especial issue for the manager of this team to consider is the interests and expectations of each member. Dissatisfaction with the Lodge, or with Freemasonry, is the major cause of resignations. Unless we reduce the high level of early resignations from our Lodges, we will not see growth in the Craft. Successful Lodges take account of these needs and interests in their planning and management, so that individual members are satisfied with their membership and grow in commitment. I address these issues in other chapters.

Other members of the care team include assistant almoners and personal mentors.

Clearly, which ever one is the manager of the care team, both the Almoner and Mentor roles require management skills and a high degree of planning and organisation as well as excellent people skills.

The final manager is the Charity Steward, who is responsible for fundraising. This role requires knowledge of Masonic charities, their purpose and the causes they support, as well as an understanding of the

Masonic festival system and local appeals. An awareness of local charitable causes also helps. Those who assist the Charity Steward, including the Stewards who sell raffle tickets, may need some briefing so that they can answer questions.

Probably the strongest skillset required by the Charity Steward is the ability to promote regular giving and to discuss doing so individually. Sending emails to ask for donations doesn't yield anywhere near as good results as the personal approach. This is a management role because, once again it requires planning and an ability to work with others, especially the Master, Secretary and Almoner.

I am a firm believer in putting square pegs into square holes. Therefore, the selection and appointment of these key officers has to be carefully planned and considered. While technically the Master has the authority to select and appoint all except the Treasurer, in practice the Lodge ought to identify who is currently best placed to occupy each role.

People perform at their best when they are both able and willing. However, not all willing volunteers are as suited as they might think to a particular position. In one of my Lodges, we had to find a new Treasurer. A former accountant, who had already messed up the finances of three other Lodges, offered to take on the role. So, rather than give a job to the first person who volunteers, the Lodge might consider who among their members has the best match to the skills and qualities required for the job. They can then check that they are willing to devote the time and energy required.

Someone in the Lodge, perhaps the Mentor or the Secretary, ought to hold discussions with members to identify their aspirations for office and suggest who will succeed the current job holder. It is very helpful for a Lodge to develop a succession plan for this purpose. A succession plan is built by considering who might have potential for each role and when they will become available. Assessing potential is done by considering each member's skills, qualities and interests. A succession plan ensures that no one holds any office for too long and that everyone is considered for roles to which they may aspire.

A lot of diplomacy is needed for such discussions. Those who are not offered the role they would ideally like can be asked to do something else that will be satisfying and agreeable to them. Willingness, remember, is as important as ability. Once completed, the plan can be shared and agreed with the Lodge.

Role turnover is key to the success of a Lodge. If any one person holds any office for too long their performance and interest will tend to decline, due to fatigue or complacency. Sometimes people who have held a role for an extended period of time become blind to changes around them and therefore "unconsciously incompetent." They do not always appreciate how their effectiveness deteriorates, to the detriment of the Lodge. Holding on to the same role for too long also prevents others from developing skills and deprives the Lodge of accumulated valuable experience. If a Lodge has three or four past Secretaries or Directors of Ceremonies, it is in a far stronger position than one which has only one of each.

Role turnover also refreshes the Lodge. It introduces new people with enthusiasm and new ideas. It enables more people to develop skills that can be used beyond the Lodge itself. It also allows such people to receive deserved recognition by their Metropolitan, Provincial or District Grand Lodge.

Of course, for a Lodge to have role turnover it needs to have a sufficient pool of talented and enthusiastic members. Indeed, the lack of talent and enthusiasm is one reason Lodges go downhill and decline in membership.

If a Lodge is experiencing difficulty finding able and willing people prepared to take on jobs, now or in the near future, it may want to consider the issues around growth and change (see chapters 4 and 7).

Throughout my professional and volunteer activities I have always made use of some core leadership and management models and principles. These have given me a framework around which I can develop my knowledge, skills and actions. They have provided a reference point for when I am considering different options. They help me develop solutions when I face difficulties.

The models I have selected in what follows are among the best established, better known and more easily remembered. There are others, some of which are more recent, and they too have great value. However, as part of my purpose in this book is to help you apply learning and experiences from other walks of life to your Lodge, I have opted to go with what are probably the best-known models.

One such model is John Adair's "Action Centred Leadership".[3] The model is simple to follow and easy to remember. It tells us that an effective leader or manager concentrates on three functions:

1. Achieving the task
2. Supporting the group
3. Developing the individual.

The best leaders devote time to each of these considerations and, if urgency pushes them to concentrate temporarily on one to the detriment of others, they can then restore the equilibrium as soon as they can.

If we apply these functions to leadership in a Lodge, the overall big task for a Master is to leave the Lodge in a better condition than at the start of their year. They may also have a small number of priorities that need to be addressed. They then have a series of smaller tasks relating to each meeting and event throughout their year.

These big and smaller tasks can all be planned around a set of annual goals and these in turn could reflect the seven habits of highly successful Lodges (see chapter 1). Some examples might be:

- Introduce new members
- Retain all of the existing members
- Increase the involvement of all members in the work of the Lodge
- Introduce some meaningful Masonic education into the programme
- Provide a range of social activities to satisfy the different interests of members and their families
- Produce a Lodge communication plan
- Review and update the Lodge plan (see the Members' Pathway).

Five to seven goals are plenty for one year. They ought to concentrate on agreed priorities and be consistent with the Lodge plan, if one is already agreed (see chapter 10). This will ensure there is long term continuity and progress rather than sharp "about turns" every year. What is essential is that the Master proposes the goals, agrees them with the others in the Lodge and then asks the managers and other members of the Lodge to plan the detail and deliver their implementation. The Master should not be trying to do the detailed planning and implementation themself.

As well as defining goals, the effective Master, in their role as leader, also advocates them, reminds members of them and encourages members to work towards them. But even this is not enough. Progress towards the achievement of goals, via the plans put in place to do so, should be monitored. Monitoring should be done by the managers, who will set up records and systems for this purpose. However, the leader – the Master in the case of a Lodge – should review the achievement of the goals and help the Lodge to celebrate success and learn valuable lessons for the future.

In chapter 10, I look at how a Lodge can develop a strategy for its future, agree goals, plan and review progress.

The second of John Adair's leadership functions is "supporting the group". Again, this can be split into big and small. The big group is the whole membership. Small groups are each of the management teams and other groups such as all the recent members or all the Past Masters. By support I really mean actions like:

- Encouraging the group(s) to fulfil their purpose
- Providing help, guidance and support to others' efforts and activities
- Recognising progress and achievements
- Helping members reach understanding and agreement
- Promoting harmony and consensus in the Lodge.

Whereas "achieving the task" is all about goals, plans and actions, "supporting the group" is all about people. It requires people skills and also the exercise of people qualities, such as patience and open-mindedness, and our Masonic virtues of respect, tolerance, fairness and integrity. A good Master is the Master for all members and avoids taking sides, at least until all views and opinions have been aired.

John Adair's third leadership function is "developing the individual". As with the second, this is about people. In practice, the Master may not have a direct role in developing all individual members of the Lodge. However, it is important that they identify those who do need assistance and makes arrangements to ensure they receive it from a suitable member or personal mentor. The Master can work with the Lodge Mentor to ensure that individual development is offered and is continuous. If the Lodge has traditionally expected all new members to follow a pre-determined path, the Master may be the one who champions a new approach based on understanding individual needs and providing personal support and development.

What is important is that the Master develops effective one-to-one working relationships with their officers and other members. Showing impartiality and fairness is important. Recognising and thanking people for their individual efforts goes a long way to people feeling valued and appreciated.

John Adair's model is primarily about leadership, but it applies also to managers within the Lodge. For example, while the Lodge Secretary's role may appear to be primarily focused on administrative tasks, the Secretary also plays a big part in supporting groups and developing individuals. This can be either directly or indirectly, depending on how the Secretary makes or steers decisions and influences the work of others. The Secretary may also be the person best placed to help an inexperienced Master fulfil their own leadership functions. For example, they might encourage the Master to concentrate on and balance the needs of the task, group and individual, or help them define goals and build relationships with the other members.

Adair's model tells us what effective leaders do, but it doesn't tell us how they ought to do them.

Alongside Adair's "Action centred leadership" model, I also find it very helpful to use a variety of different leadership or management styles when asking others to do something. A leadership or management style is concerned with <u>how</u> we do something rather than <u>what</u> we do. A very useful and widely applied model of leadership and management styles, one developed by Paul Hersey & Ken Blanchard, looks at the amount of direction and support the leader or manager gives to others.[4]

Direction here tends to relate to decisions. A directive leader or manager makes decisions and issues instructions. A non-directive leader leaves the decisions to others, within defined and agreed boundaries. A supportive leader puts time into encouraging and assisting others to do what they are meant to do. A non-supportive leader leaves them to it, although they might seek help if they think they need it.

Putting these together, we can identify four different simple leadership styles:

1. Directing (in which the leader or manager makes the decisions, communicates them and leaves other people to implement them).
2. Coaching (in which the leader or manager might still make the decisions but explains their thinking to others to help them learn how to decide).
3. Supporting (in which the leader or manager encourages others to make decisions and helps them through the process).
4. Delegating (in which the leader or manager defines boundaries and allows others to make and implement decisions within those boundaries, providing support only when needed or requested).

I should make the point that the labels given to these four styles do not have the same meaning as the same words in other contexts. For example, in the wider use of the term, delegation is a management process in its own right, not just a leadership style.

According to Hersey & Blanchard, the effective or skilled leader adjusts their style, selecting one depending on the needs of the situation and the people being led or managed. Generally speaking, the less able people are, the more direction they need. The less willing they are, the more support they need.

So, for example, the directive style is often used when people are new to a situation, when they are willing but not very able. It is also used in an emergency situation to issue instructions to minimise risk or damage.

To give an example of how styles can change, imagine a leader or manager is working to develop another person's decision making. They might first demonstrate how they make decisions. Then they coach the other person through some approaches, encouraging them to make their own decisions. As they gain experience, they adjust their style to a more "light touch" supportive approach. Finally, when they have confidence in the other person, they allow them to make decisions without their intervention.

If we apply this to situations in a Lodge, there should rarely be any need for a directive style, except perhaps when a major ceremonial event is about to happen, and time is of the essence. Nevertheless, the directive style was commonly used by many senior brethren at a time when members were perhaps more deferential. Nowadays, members are much less likely to accept being told what has been decided by others and what they are expected to do.

The coaching style is often useful in Lodge situations, and especially when people are learning a new role, office, or piece of ritual. It does take some effort and requires both knowledge of the subject in hand and a lot of skill in encouraging people. Mentors often start with this style and gradually move to a supporting style as the other person becomes more capable and confident. Equally, outgoing officers will find this approach – starting with the coaching style and gradually moving to the supporting style – very useful as a way of helping their successor take up the reins. In fact, in some Lodges the outgoing Secretary or Director of Ceremonies acts as the Assistant for one or two years so that they can provide this coaching and support.

The ultimate is to be able to use the delegating style with the highly able and willing. The wise Secretary will know the strengths and interests of individual members. If they and the other senior members can help develop those strengths and interests, the Lodge will get the best out of its members and will be able to rely upon them to take on a job and do it well. As with all voluntary organisations, the Lodge's strength will depend to a large extent on the number of willing members and their range of capabilities.

In their leadership role, the Master will have lots of opportunities to use different styles during their term. On some – hopefully rare – occasions they may wish to assert their will and be directive. On others they will encourage others to make decisions. Equally, they will find the coaching and supportive styles appropriate with different people. If a Master did not adjust their style, they would probably find they are perceived as either too controlling, at one extreme, or too weak, at the other.

Back in the world of work, one of the major shifts in the last thirty years has been towards working in teams. Organisations have discovered that teamwork generates loyalty, commitment and a drive for high achievement. Understanding and applying the principles of teamwork, and especially of high-performance teams, can also help us in our Lodges.

I am not using the word teams in the everyday, even flippant, sense commonly adopted by game show hosts. A team in not a loose collection of people who come together briefly at a point in time.

A team is a tight knit unit which has been through a demanding developmental process to become something quite special. A high-performance team is made up of people with diverse but complementary skills and qualities. They share the same goals and work together to deliver those goals, putting the team and its achievement above individual egos.

A great example of this was the 1966 England football team that won the World Cup. The team manager, Alf Ramsey, did not assemble individual stars and leave them to it. He assembled players who would mesh together and put the good of the team above their own ambitions. He then trained them together for longer than any of his predecessors had ever done, so that they knew and could "play off" each other's strengths and weaknesses.

Another example is Nelson's approach to sea battles. He kept his ships at sea, training the crews to follow instructions and load and discharge guns in rapid fire. He also briefed his Captains, his "band of brothers" on the strategy for each battle so that they could each play their part and make decisions within the boundaries of that strategy. When it came to battle itself, Nelson's ships fired at a far superior rate than his opponents.

A high-performance team develops its own norms, its own methods of working, its own team spirit, its own rituals and its own ways of celebrating success. In fact, such is the bond that can develop in such teams that one of their challenges is to admit and accept new team members.

Such levels of achievement require the team to go through a tough learning process. The process has been described by Bruce Tuckman & Mary Ann Jensen.[5] In summary it involves a number of stages:

1 *Forming*, a generally polite phase during which team members get to know each other, size each other up, work out the roles in the team and clarify their overall purpose together.
2 *Storming*, during which the team experiences friction and sometimes full conflict as different personalities jockey for position and work out each other's strengths and weaknesses before they adjust to and accept each other.

3 *Norming*, during which the team develops its own identity and unique "ways we do things here", or "norms".
4 *Performing*, during which the team polishes its ways of working together and reaches its potential as a high-performance team.
5 *Adjourning*, at which point the team splits, having fulfilled its purpose or otherwise, and individual members move on, often with promises of nostalgic reunions.

What can a Lodge learn from an understanding of true teamwork?

First, that this is what many new members hope for or expect when they join a new social group. It is especially the case in Freemasonry that many joining are looking to be part of a "band of brothers." The language of teamwork is now deeply embedded in employing organisations. Freemasonry has not traditionally used this language but perhaps we should now look to do so.

Secondly, if a Lodge is to have an enduring future, having good leaders and good managers in the right place is not enough. Developing a team approach within the Lodge will help the busy team managers (ie, the Secretary, Director of Ceremonies, the Almoner or Mentor and the Charity Steward) share their workload, develop eventual successors and deliver great Freemasonry for more members.

Thirdly, the Master and the various managers in the Lodge ought themselves to work as one team. Differences and difficulties between these officers can create friction and tension within the Lodge. If the managers work together, support the Master in their capacity as leader and align their work, Lodge meetings and other activities are far more likely to go smoothly and harmoniously.

Finally, teams can become cliques. This is the downside of teamwork and is something that needs to be avoided. Otherwise, it will be difficult for new members to find a place in the team and this in turn often leads to stagnation and decline. Teams do need to be refreshed with new members. They then need to be flexible enough to accommodate new ideas and approaches, so that they continue to evolve.

In summary, understanding the different roles, tasks and approaches of leaders and managers can help Lodges work more effectively. Adopting a team approach to the management of the Lodge will help all officers and members do their tasks as well as is possible, for the benefit of all.

Having addressed the matter of who leads and who manages in a Lodge, in the next chapter I consider the – sometimes – challenging issue of decision making in a Lodge, and offer an approach that both suits our constitutions and a modern approach to Lodge management.

---

[1] Awards include National Training Awards and Best Factory Awards. Accreditations include the Institute of Leadership and Management and the Institute of Training & Occupational Learning.

[2] Published in "Introducing the Success Cycle: Six steps to achieving your dreams", Carrfields Publications, 2018.

[3] John Adair (1973), "Action Centred Leadership", McGraw-Hill, New York.

[4] Paul Hersey & Ken Blanchard (1982), "Management and organisational behaviour: utilising human resources." Prentice-Hall, New Jersey.

[5] Bruce Tuckman & Mary Ann Jensen (1977), "Stages of small-group development revisited." Group & Organization Studies, 2(4), pp 419–427.

Chapter 6

Who Decides?

One of the key issues I have had to address throughout my time developing leaders in different organisations has been understanding what authority a manager has for making decisions. Another has been the process a group (such as a board, department or project team) can follow to make "good quality" decisions after they have generated, considered and evaluated different options.

The first issue is partly to do with an organisation's formal decision-making framework, defined by its governing documents and rules, and partly to do with the informal practices that develop over time, sometimes in contravention of the rules. This issue is so important that the manner in which decisions are made helps define the culture of the organisation, "the way we do things around here."

As for the second issue, there is an excellent decision-making approach that I have used for many years and which captures options, considers their merits and arrives at a balanced and well thought out decision. It fits in very well with how our Lodges function.

In this chapter I will suggest how a Lodge, its officers and members, may create decision making practises that promote the health and strength of the Lodge and avoid the difficulties that can arise from poor decision making. To achieve this, I first need to explain some aspects of our formal decision-making processes. However, I will not duplicate the comprehensive guidance available in the Book of Constitutions and elsewhere. If you want further details on these matters, I encourage you to obtain a copy of VW Bro. Graham Redman's excellent book, "Masonic Etiquette Today", as well as the Book of Constitutions.[1,2]

Formal decision-making processes

The governing documents for an organisation define how decisions may be made and who may participate in them. They define any limits to authority so that decisions are known to be legitimate. When decisions are made outside of the limits defined by these frameworks they can result in dissent and discord. In a voluntary membership organisation such as a Lodge they can lead to loss of support and ultimately to resignations. In fact, poor decision making by the wrong people is often the root cause of problems within a Lodge.

The governing documents for Lodges under United Grand Lodge of England are:

1   The Rules contained in the Book of Constitutions
2   Lodge By-laws.

In addition, every recommendation of the Board of General Purposes that is adopted by Grand Lodge becomes an edict binding on all Lodges and brethren. In many cases these have been included in the booklet, "Information for the Guidance of Members of the Craft". This is presented to every Initiate and every Installed Master at the appropriate ceremony.

Every Lodge defines by-laws according to a framework laid down by Grand Lodge. Lodge by-laws must then be formally adopted by the Lodge and approved by or on behalf of Grand Lodge. By-laws create local rules particular to that Lodge, which it is then obliged to work within. By-laws are subservient to the rules and edicts of Grand Lodge and cannot override the provisions they contain.

Royal Arch Chapters are governed by the Regulations of Supreme Grand Chapter, contained in the Book of Constitutions. Every recommendation of the Committee of General Purposes that is adopted by Supreme Grand Chapter becomes a binding edict. As with Lodges, Chapters define, adopt and have approved their by-laws in a similar manner to that used by Lodges.

There are occasions a Lodge may wish, for legitimate reasons, to act outside of a rule or by-law. On such occasions they must obtain a dispensation in advance from the Grand Master (for acting outside of the rules laid down by the Book of Constitutions) or their Metropolitan, Provincial or District Grand Master (for acting outside of their by-laws).

Before being Installed into the chair of their Lodge, the Master Elect is required to "submit to and promise to support" a summary of the Antient Charges and Regulations. These require the Master Elect to:

1   Abide by the laws of the country in which they reside
2   Submit to the "awards and resolutions" of their brethren "in general Lodge convened"

3 Remain neutral in the matter of "private piques and quarrels"
4 Pay homage to the Grand Master (ie, to respect and show allegiance to their authority)
5 Strictly to conform to every Edict of the Grand Lodge
6 Gain the consent of Grand Lodge before attempting to make any alteration to the "Body of Masonry"
7 Abide by the rules governing the forming of Lodges, the Initiation of candidates and the admission of visitors, so as to ensure the Lodge continues to be "regular" in its actions.

Shortly afterwards, while making their obligation as Master Elect, they promise to enforce a "due obedience to those Charges and Regulations".

In these two acts they are acknowledging that their authority is formally defined, bound and limited by the rules and edicts of Grand Lodge. Following their Installation, they are presented with a copy of the Book of Constitutions and of the by-laws of their Lodge, often with the injunction that it is their duty to enforce these. Then, during the Address to the Master, they are reminded that they should strictly observe "the by-laws of your Lodge, the Constitutions of Masonry" and above all the Sacred Writings. Rule 114 of the Book of Constitutions confirms that, "The Master is responsible for the due observance of the laws by the Lodge over which he presides".

Therefore, at numerous points our ritual and practices inform and remind us that we are obliged to act within the rules laid down by Grand Lodge.

So, how does a Master comply with their duty to enforce these rules?

First, they should read the rules and by-laws themself, at least as they relate to Private Lodges. Secondly, they should appoint a Secretary who has a good working knowledge of the rules and who is able to guide them through the various requirements. They will benefit from such advice in open Lodge, at committee and in the day-to-day functioning of the Lodge.

Let us consider decision making in each of the above three scenarios in a little more detail.

The Lodge has authority

Except where explicitly stated in the Book of Constitutions or the Lodge by-laws, the Master has very little personal decision-making authority. The Lodge regulates its own proceedings, within the bounds of the Book of Constitutions (Rule 155), and the Master is required to submit to the "awards and resolutions" (ie, decisions) of their brethren. All brethren in turn are expected to make a "ready acquiescence in all votes and resolutions duly passed by a majority of the brethren".

In effect, the Lodge is its own executive body. No person or committee can make decisions that should be made by the Lodge. The only way the brethren can exercise their collective decision-making authority is by voting in a properly convened and opened Lodge. This became clear during the Covid-19 pandemic when United Grand Lodge (and therefore Supreme Grand Chapter) required votes to be made in an open Lodge by brethren who were gathered in person in the same physical space and not over a video-conferencing platform.

The manner in which votes may be made is laid down by the rules and varies for different decisions. Some votes require a secret ballot. Some may be made by a show of hands. Some require a simple majority while others require a higher percentage of the members present. A vote relating to the admission of new members requires three or fewer dissenters, as defined in the Lodge by-laws. In advance of any meeting where a vote is to be taken, the wise Secretary will consult the Book of Constitutions and the Lodge by-laws to check on the procedure to be followed.

Some decisions require prior notice before a vote can be taken. This is so that brethren can be informed in advance, ask questions, seek further information and give the matter proper consideration. In such cases the proposal is included in written form on the summons for the meeting.

Some Lodges require that brethren give a "notice of motion" at one meeting before they can propose that motion at the next. The "notice of motion" is then included on the summons for the follow up meeting. The Book of Constitutions only requires Lodges to use such a "notice of motion" in the case of a proposal to "remove" the Lodge to another meeting place (Rule 141). Nevertheless, many Lodges also use oral "notices of motion" for charity donations and other major expenditure. This has the advantage of ensuring there are no surprises and that everyone has a chance to express an opinion. The downside is that it can slow down the disbursement of charitable funds for worthy causes.

Providing brethren have sufficient notice before a vote is taken and the rules are followed, formal decision making in the Lodge normally presents few difficulties. The system is open, transparent and robust.

It is when we come to committees, whether formal or informal, and the authority of individual officers, that difficulties over decision making can often occur.

What about committees?

Some committees assume or take to themselves powers for decision-making that they do not actually possess.

Rule 154 is the only reference in the Book of Constitutions to Lodge Committees. It defines the purpose of a Lodge Committee as considering and reporting on proposals for membership. It stipulates that "no Committee can be invested with any general executive powers." It also says that a Lodge may, by resolution, refer any other matters to a committee for consideration and report, "with power to act within such limits as the Lodge may define".

Therefore, properly convened full meetings of the Lodge, and all its members present, always retain authority for making Lodge decisions. No Lodge committee is empowered to make any decisions on behalf of the Lodge, unless specifically authorised to do so by a resolution passed in open Lodge. And no committee can be given carte blanche authority – or general executive powers – over Lodge matters.

Strictly speaking, the outcomes of votes in Lodge committees should be put to the Lodge as recommendations for the brethren to endorse, or otherwise, just as the Board of General Purposes puts its recommendations to Quarterly Communications of Grand Lodge for approval.

Nevertheless, many Lodge committees do act as decision making bodies and assume an authority that should be exercised by the Lodge as a whole. This often arises because Lodge committees comprise the Past Masters and senior officers. While these members have more experience of Freemasonry, they do not have a monopoly on good ideas, opportunities or solutions. In fact, committees made up only of more experienced people can tend to stick to the familiar and reject the novel or innovative. Sometimes senior members use the Lodge committee to exercise their will over the Lodge. This disenfranchises other members whose opinion should be sought, whose voice should be heard and whose vote should be counted. It has led to resignations from brethren who believe what we tell them, namely that we are all equal, but who actually experience something rather different.

I referred above to "informal committees". These do not appear anywhere in the Book of Constitutions or in Lodge by-laws. In effect, they are self-appointed groups of members who make decisions and – sometimes – impose their will on the Lodge. The first other members may hear about such decisions is when an announcement is made in a Lodge meeting, often as a fait accompli. These informal committees can exercise great power over major issues in Lodges – such as the appointment of key officers.

In some Lodges, such "informal committees" are quite acceptable. Sometimes the members accept that certain members are well positioned to make certain decisions. Or they realise that certain benevolent autocrats are willing to put in effort where they are not. However, as the system is far from transparent it can lead to problems if members of these informal committees overstep the mark and exceed their implicit authority. In these cases, members often resign rather than "make waves".

This is where we move into the area of Lodge culture, or "how we normally do things here" (see Chapter 9). Culture varies from Lodge to Lodge and develops over time. A closed culture is one where decisions are made by a few and imposed on the many. An open culture is one in which decisions are made by the many, often after consultation and consensus building.

Many Lodges are run by some or all of the Past Masters who make decisions in a closed manner, despite the formal rules and structures laid down in the Book of Constitutions. They justify this by suggesting that members require a certain amount of experience of Freemasonry before they can make a useful contribution. This practice is less acceptable to the newer members joining in the 21st century. As I explained in chapter three, such members expect to have their contribution valued and for them to be included in decision making processes. If they feel disenfranchised, they are more likely to leave.

In recognition of this change, more and more Lodges are opening out their decision-making processes and including all members in their consideration of issues. Some have reduced the number of their committee meetings. Some use the committee only to plan Installation meetings or to produce recommendations and proposals for the Lodge itself to consider and endorse. Others have opened committee meetings out to all members so that a wider range of opinions and ideas can be considered. Many ensure that all members receive copies of the minutes of Lodge committee meetings. Some Lodges use more informal meetings open to all members. These meetings act as discussion forums to conduct Lodge reviews and build Lodge plans – including succession plans – as suggested in the Members' Pathway.

These more open approaches do more than help newer members feel valued and included. They also make their skills, experience, creativity and enthusiasm available to the Lodge at an earlier stage. This may be disconcerting or threatening to traditionalists within the Lodge, who might resist changes that are proposed as a result. I shall return to this issue in chapter 7.

Open culture organisations are more conducive to harmony. In these organisations, members are consulted before decisions are made and have the opportunity to contribute ideas and to debate options. When the decision is actually voted upon, any dissent or contrary views are likely to have already been identified and addressed beforehand.

This brings me to consensus-based decisions as opposed to democratic decisions.

By democracy, I mean the practice of majority voting. This is a great system for electing and running governments where, over time, it provides balance between opposite positions. However, it is less effective for smaller groups of people. In these, majority voting can result in a large minority being unhappy with the outcome. For example, in a group of eleven voters, a vote of six in favour of and five against a motion will leave five being less than content. If the issue is fundamental to that group, that may be sufficient cause for those who lost the vote to leave the group.

Imagine a Lodge wishing to vote on a change of meeting dates or on a matter of principle or policy. A significant minority could feel so unhappy with the outcome that they resign. Such issues have been known to split Lodges.

An alternative is to reach consensus before a formal vote is taken. Consensus involves all members, or at least an acceptable large proportion of members, agreeing to a decision or course of action. It often starts with a consultation process, to gather, share and evaluate ideas. Consensus almost always requires compromise and the sacrifice of ideal outcomes before a consensus can be reached. While no one person may get "all their own way", the act of compromise requires a respect for others and a "meeting of minds" so that what is eventually decided gets "buy-in" and support from everyone. Consultation and consensus are also very good ways to address resistance to change, which I shall examine in more detail in chapter 7.

Consensus is an informal decision-making process. If necessary, it can be ratified by a formal vote, which will normally result in a larger majority than if consensus had not been built beforehand.

Day to day functioning of the Lodge

It is in the day-to-day functioning of the Lodge that we often see another example of poor decision making. This arises when one or more officers act beyond the authority granted to them by the rules or by-laws, or beyond what is expected by the Master and brethren.

The plus side of this is that the officers concerned are being decisive. The downside is that it doesn't take long for other members to be excluded from decisions. Some members don't mind this at all. Some are quite content for others to take on the work involved, to make decisions and to be the driving force. However, this can also start a slippery slope in which the wider membership avoids its responsibilities for the Lodge and sit back while others do everything. This is not good for the Lodge's long-term health, which is better promoted by involving more people and sharing the work.

In such cases, the remedy is for another member or members of the Lodge to address this directly with the person concerned. However, I have seen many examples of some reticence for doing this. It is often the case that the people concerned don't wish to upset the person who has overstepped the mark. They fear it may cause disharmony in the Lodge. However, it amazes me that so many brethren who have apparently had successful management careers, and therefore should be quite capable of dealing with these issues properly and with sensitivity, seem to be unwilling to address them. Unfortunately, unless such issues are dealt with promptly, they tend to cause even worse problems for the Lodge as the officer increases his influence unchecked.

The solution involves practising a very important management skill. This is to give corrective feedback in a calm, supportive and objective – rather than personal – manner. The technique is in four stages. First to point out the inappropriate behaviour and the basis for it being wrong, always sticking to observable facts. Then to explain the negative impact or outcome it has on the Lodge. Next is to describe the concerns expressed by members. Finally, to detail a better approach or different behaviours that should replace what has been happening. These four stages should flow as part of a two-way discussion. They are most effective when the person giving the feedback has a good relationship with the person receiving it.

Creativity, options and decisions

As I mentioned in the introduction, another issue around decision making is how a group, such as a Lodge or a committee, arrive at a good quality decision.

The challenge is that many groups – such as committees – move very quickly to decide a course of action after considering only a few alternatives. This often arises as a result of "serial consideration" in which each idea or proposed solution is discussed and evaluated as it arises. People take a view on each option and align themselves for or against them. The first option that secures general support is often selected.

Unfortunately, early ideas are rarely the best ideas. They tend to be the most obvious, the most familiar or most comfortable. Rarely do early ideas break new ground or provide innovative and creative solutions.

A popular technique for overcoming this is brainstorming. This suspends judgement until lots of ideas are "on the table." The group members generate ideas by offering whatever thoughts come to mind. Each idea triggers new thoughts in others. To work effectively, brainstorming requires those involved to follow some simple rules, such as no comments are allowed until all ideas have been expressed. It normally works best when a skilled facilitator leads the process.

The group then filters the results of their brainstorming session using acceptance criteria they agree. Criteria might cover, for example, the cost, effort required, simplicity or speed of implementation. Finally, they consider and evaluate the ideas or options that make it through the filtering process. Unfortunately, brainstorming often fails through poor facilitation, poor compliance with the rules or poor selection of criteria.

Another approach is called "decision thinking". It is a four-stage process, as follows:

1 *Define the question and gather the information*

   The group define the issue as a question. For example, "What is the best way of rehearsing a ceremony?" The precise question needs to be well thought through. It must not oversimplify the issues.

   Once the group has decided the question, it can gather relevant background information.

2 *Create Alternatives*

   The group generates a range of possible answers to the question. They may use the first stage of brainstorming for this purpose.

   If the alternatives are not judged to be very good, they reconsider the question or go back and change it. Decision-thinking is not always a linear process. It is acceptable to go backwards before moving forwards.

3 *Predict the Consequences*

   The group considers each alternative answer to the question, identifies all the possible outcomes and predicts their consequences. This may involve a degree of "educated guessing". The relevant information, gathered during stage 1, can help evaluate these consequences.

   This stage involves assessing the possible benefits as well as the risks. It also helps the group generate contingency plans.

   Once again, it is allowable to backtrack to earlier stages. But once the group has gone back to a particular stage, it should work forward through each subsequent stage in sequence.

4 *Reach the Decision*

Finally, the group makes a value judgement to determine the best course of action, given the alternatives and their consequences.

Even at this stage it is possible to go back and work through any or all of the stages again.

The decision thinking process can be time consuming when first used. It can also be frustrating for those who have a vested interest in an early idea. However, with practice it gets easier. It is an inclusive process that tends to build support for new ideas and commitment to the eventual decision. It works well as part of a consensus building approach. Most importantly, it provides a decision-making framework that combines creative thinking, analysis and evaluation, resulting in better quality and enduring decisions.

Summary

The formal processes detailed in the Book of Constitutions provide a robust system for a Lodge to make decisions. However, in many cases Lodge committees, cliques and officers make decisions without fully consulting members or without building consensus. In the 21st century, members increasingly expect to be involved in Lodge decision making and to have their contributions heard and considered. Consensus building is a helpful process which, along with the generation, consideration and evaluation of many different options, can result in increased buy-in and support for decisions. All this helps promote the health and strength of the Lodge.

---

[1] Graham Redman (2009), "Masonic Etiquette Today", Ian Allan Publishing.
[2] UGLE (2020), "Constitutions of the Antient Fraternity of Free and Accepted Masons under the United Grand Lodge of England" (The Book of Constitutions), UGLE, London.

Chapter 7

But they Don't Want to Change

By now you may be concerned that there are some members of your Lodge who might resist or block some of the evolutionary changes you and others may wish to make. This leads to the question, "How can we overcome or address resistance to change from others?" It is one of the most popular questions that arises when I deliver talks to Lodges and it often comes up on social media.

In chapter 4 I explained how evolution and change have always been features of Freemasonry and why they must continue to be so if we are to survive and thrive. The issue in this chapter is how to address resistance to change when a minority of members hinder the decisions that a majority wish to make.

It is clear that, in some Lodges and Chapters, influential members sometimes delay or even block changes. Some Lodges take the view that the status quo is the least risky and so, for the apparent sake of harmony, they give in to the few. However, they then run the risk of alienating those who wish to move the Lodge forward.

So, what can we do to persuade such brethren of the need to evolve and to support specific changes? How can we address such resistance to change and secure the willing support of more members?

In this chapter I will:

1. examine why some people resist change,
2. outline six general approaches to managing resistance to change, and
3. consider some relevant, perhaps typical, situations encountered in Freemasonry and how they can be addressed.

What follows is an everyday explanation of research from the fields of psychology, management and organisational development and my own experience dealing with these issues as a professional consultant, board level facilitator and coach as well as in my capacity as a Freemason. I have included references in the footnotes for those who want more in depth explanations.

Why do some people resist change?

I often hear people say, "No one likes change". While it is certainly true that some people don't like change, it is also clear that many people thrive on it. The difference seems to come down to whether people think they will gain or lose something from the change.

Generally, those who resist change don't want to lose something that is important to them. Those who want to drive change recognise personal or collective benefits to be had from the change.

Understanding what people think they will gain or lose as a result of proposed changes is the key to addressing resistance to change.

Rational and emotional responses

A person's resistance to change can involve both rational and emotional responses. The case for a change may make logical sense. Equally, logical arguments may also be put forward to resist the same change. In addition, a proposed change often results in emotional responses from people, whether in favour or against.

Those who study the psychology of personality[1] recognise that some people focus more on rational or logical thinking and others focus more on emotional elements or responses. Therefore, when we think about how we address resistance to change, we need to anticipate and understand both rational and emotional responses.

Types of resistance

Researchers have suggested there are four main reasons[2] people resist change, as follows:

1 *Parochial self-interest*

   This type of resistance arises when people expect the change to result in some form of personal loss and put their own needs and interests above those of the wider group or organisation.

2 *Misunderstanding and lack of trust*

A misunderstanding of the change, its rationale, process, result or benefits, can trigger resistance to change. This is especially true when there is poor communication or a lack of trust between the parties involved.

3 *Different assessments*

Resistance may come when a person (or group of people) assesses a situation, the reasons for change or the suggested approach to the change differently from those who are proposing the change. They are likely to come to a different conclusion or solution. It is always possible that they may have information that the proposers don't. They may even have a better solution and could come up with an improved proposal.

4 *Low tolerance*

When change is slow or non-existent, people tend to become familiar and comfortable with, "the way things are done around here." Often, they then believe, "we have always done it this way", even when that is not the case. When a change is then proposed or introduced some people fear they will not be able to adapt or that the new reality won't be as comfortable for them. This resistance is often found among some of our elderly or longest serving members, for whom Freemasonry represents a comfortable constant in their lives. Even when the change promises rational benefits, it can be resisted simply because the very effort to make the change is perceived as too much.

Driving and restraining forces[3]

A popular approach to managing change is to look at what are known as driving and restraining forces.

Driving forces are all those things (ie, issues, actions, beliefs, potential benefits, etc) that are in favour of a change. Restraining forces are those things (ie, objections, actions, fears, pitfalls, losses) which are holding back change. When driving forces are stronger than the restraining forces, change happens. When restraining forces are stronger than driving forces, any moves for change can be delayed. When some people want change and others don't, frustration can build.

We can use an understanding of driving and restraining forces to develop solutions. For example, we can:

a) increase the strength of the driving forces (eg, improve the argument for and benefits of change)
b) reduce the strength of the restraining forces (eg, address the concerns and reassure objectors)
c) a combination of both approaches.

The "change curve"

The change curve is a way of looking at how people's responses to change can vary and develop over time. There tends to be typical patterns of response to expected and unexpected change. By understanding these we can plan a change process to improve how we manage change.

Our initial response to an unexpected change is often emotional. It is often shock, followed by denial, then anger and even depression.[4] These emotional responses against a change tend to give way eventually to acceptance and more rational responses that can range from cautious experimentation through to acting as a "change champion".

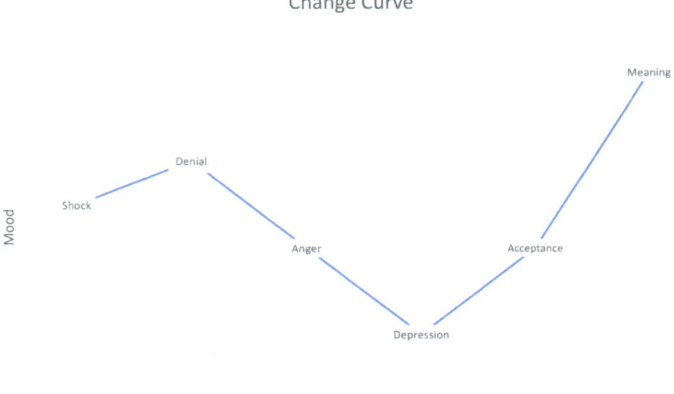

Graph 2: The change curve

How we respond to change resistance should take account of a person's position along this change curve, recognising that the same person may change their perspective over time.

When people expect the change, when they have time to think about it and adjust, the initial responses tend to be more accepting. We can build on this tendency by discussing the reasons for change and listen to what people have to say, before we agree and plan what will actually change. Introducing a change with little warning, decided upon by a few members rather than by the whole, is more likely to result in an emotional reaction against the change.

Change types

Some people have developed a pattern of behaviour, or way they typically respond, towards change. We call these typical patterns, "change types". The following looks at four "change types" and ways in which we can encourage those who respond with each to adopt a more favourable approach to change.

The approach considers two dimensions; positive and negative responses to change, and action verses inaction. We can use the approach to help people move towards a positive and active response.

	Inaction	*Action*
Positive attitude	'YES' PEOPLE "I would if ...", "I could if ..."	CHANGE CHAMPIONS "I will ... ", "I can ..."
Negative attitude	VICTIMS "I won't ...", "I can't ..."	CHANGE TERRORISTS "It won't ...", "It can't ..."

Table 3: Change types

1 *Change Champions*

   These have a positive attitude and a willingness to try and to take action. Typically, they:
   a) Identify with the positive benefits or opportunities of change
   b) Recognise a change as a challenge

c) Are open to and willing to learn
d) Stretch their personal comfort zones.

2 *Yes People*

These appear to have a positive attitude towards change, but do not follow through with action. Often they say the right thing but do not contribute to change. They may:
a) Agree that change is needed but are unwilling to change themselves
b) Deny that change is needed in themselves
c) Hope that the change won't impact upon them
d) Avoid taking risks.

To become a "Change Champion", "Yes People" need to:
a) Work to simple, step-by-step, targets
b) Deliver short time-scale outcomes that involve some change
c) Build their confidence
d) Get regular supportive feedback.

3 *Change Terrorists*

These people have a high level of activity, but it is focused towards negative or counter-productive outcomes. They may talk a lot, but they are critical and negative in what they say. Typically, they:
a) Identify the negative aspects of change
b) Criticise plans, ideas and the people involved
c) Are backward looking or past orientated
d) Seek supporters
e) Undermine the work of others.

To become a "Change Champion", a "Change Terrorist" needs to:
a) Listen more to other peoples' opinions
b) Express their concerns in a more constructive manner
c) Recognise that change is natural
d) Recognise how past changes have had a positive impact.

4 *Victims*

Victims have both a negative attitude towards change and a lack of drive. They are less vocal than "Change Terrorists", although they can lower morale by their demeanour. When they do express themselves, it is as a passive victim who has had things done to them. Typically, they:
a) Bury their heads into the sand
b) Do the minimum required of them
c) Fail to give ideas real consideration.

To become a "Change Champion", a "Victim" needs to:
a) Recognise the effect they have on others
b) Concentrate on doing something positive, that makes use of their strengths
c) Get involved in a successful change
d) Respond to help and feedback.

Approaches to change resistance

Researchers have suggested six broad approaches[5] that we can use to address resistance to change:

1 *Education and communication*

Prior communication, explanation and education can prepare people for a change and can prompt more rational and less emotional responses. As we know from the change curve, people who are well prepared for and anticipate change tend to react with less shock, denial or anger when the change is introduced. This approach is generally the most useful and is especially so when there is a lack of information about, or understanding of, the need for change.

2 *Participation and involvement*

In general, the more people affected by a change can be involved in the change process, the better.

This approach is especially useful when potential resistance might derail the change process or when others have important information necessary for the change plan. By involving those who are likely to resist the change in the change process itself, they are more likely to buy-in and champion the change.

3 *Facilitation and support*

Some people struggle to accept or adjust to change, largely because the change will make their known and familiar world now unknown or unfamiliar.

When this happens in Freemasonry, their needs are similar to those of a new Freemason (although it may not be wise to suggest that to them). Just as mentoring helps the new Freemason adjust to and integrate with Freemasonry – and become part of it – so can providing personal support and encouragement to those who are uncomfortable with a change reassure them and allay any resistance based on their fear of loss.

4 *Negotiation and agreement*

When those resisting change are influential or hold power, negotiating key aspects of the change and offering incentives can win their support. This may slow the change process, but it will ensure it still progresses.

5 *Co-option*

Co-opting those who resist change onto the group which is planning or managing the change can secure their co-operation. This could be perceived as manipulative or patronising, so it needs to be a genuinely inclusive process rather than just a symbolic gesture.

6 *Explicit and implicit coercion*

This approach uses power and authority to force through a change. It is a traditional approach that was formerly used a great deal to manage change in organisations. It is used much less often nowadays and is much less acceptable in 21st century membership organisations. It can still have value when speed of change is important, but it carries risks of increased resistance, resentment and disengagement. If used it should be with great caution.

Situations in Freemasonry

Resistance to change comes in many forms in our Lodges. In the following I describe a few typical situations you may come across, along with some approaches that you might find useful. In all these cases, you are most likely to reduce resistance using education and communication. You can use these to establish the need for change, to legitimise it and to prepare people for what is coming.

1 *A member believes Freemasonry and his Lodge should not change.*

Some of our long-standing members joined Freemasonry at a time when there seemed to be little change. What change they did experience was probably very slow. They may now believe it is wrong to change the way the Lodge operates. They may consider the work of their predecessors to have been intended for all time. Some may even believe that the practices and traditions with which they are familiar have their origins much further back than is actually the case.

The resistance they present is an example of *misunderstanding* (see "Types of resistance", above) and may cause considerable tension or distress. It may be accompanied by a fear that a new generation is harming the Craft. Overcoming such resistance can take considerable time and patience.

A good approach is to remind these members about the history of Freemasonry over the last 300 plus years, to demonstrate that it has continually evolved over this time. The problem is that the pace of change slowed after the Second World War until more recently. Therefore, some longer serving members feel uncomfortable with evolution and change. This approach is an example of using *education and communication* (see "Approaches to change resistance", above) to address resistance.

It may also help to explain that our predecessors made their decisions based on the circumstances of their time and that we need to do the same, to safeguard the future of the Lodge. In doing this, we would be using *facilitation and support,* but we should be careful not to come across as patronising.

2 *A member misunderstands the scope of the change.*

The changes being considered by most Lodges, by Metropolitan / Provincial / District Grand Lodges and by UGLE itself, are about the way we organise and manage ourselves. They cover the organisational aspects of our Lodge practices, communication methods, decision-making, education, planning, administration and traditions. They are not about our purpose, ritual or any of the elements covered by the Ancient Charges or the Aims and Relationships of the Craft, both of which are defined in the Book of Constitutions and which are enduring and unlikely to change.

If members do not recognise and accept the distinction between organisational aspects and those concerned with our purpose, landmarks or ritual then they may *misunderstand* changes that are being proposed. Once again, misunderstanding may cause considerable tension or distress. It may be accompanied by a fear Freemasonry is losing its purpose or direction.

As with scenario one above, *education* is an effective approach, accompanied by clarification and reassurance.

3 *A member disagrees with the case for change or with the proposed change.*

A common situation in any proposed change is to meet resistance based on rational disagreement. The disagreement might be with the argument put forward to justify the change or with the proposed plan for change itself.

This is an example of the third type of resistance, *different assessment*. It is relatively easy to address through *participation and involvement,* and possibly *negotiation and agreement,* unless it is accompanied by other types of resistance, including those with an emotional basis.

It is possible that the member who is disagreeing with what is proposed has information that would change the grounds on which the change is based. *Involving* such a member in the change process will normally resolve the disagreement.

4 *A member fears the Lodge will change beyond recognition.*

Long-serving members tend to have a deep attachment to their Lodge. It may have seen them through some difficult periods in their life, as well as good ones. It may represent a constant in an increasingly bewildering and uncomfortable world. Such members are unlikely to want to lose those features of the Lodge that are meaningful and comfortable to them.

This is an example of the fourth type of resistance, *low tolerance* to change. Forcing through a change could make such members very uncomfortable and is likely to meet with strong resistance.

A useful approach is through *negotiation and agreement.* This involves asking the members to stretch – not break – the limits of their "comfort zone." In return the Lodge demonstrates respect for – and continues with – something that is important to them, but which does not threaten the health of the Lodge.

It is useful to ask such members what they consider to be the Lodge's important features, the "red lines" beyond which they do not wish to go in any change process. Such a discussion might even highlight issues that they think are ready to be changed.

Respecting the wishes of such members will often secure their support. In time, once they have established new boundaries to their comfort zones, they may well be willing to go further, support other changes and even relax their own red lines. However, they are likely to want to see that change is being well and respectfully managed before relaxing their positions.

In summary, understand the boundaries to members' comfort zones and, through *negotiation and agreement,* stretch but don't break them.

5 *A member fears they will be out of their depth or shown up as inadequate.*

If a change requires new knowledge or skills, such as when new technology is introduced, this can expose or highlight the "conscious or unconscious incompetence"[6] of members. Some may greet this as an opportunity to learn something new while others may feel inadequate, uncomfortable, insecure or may fear a loss of status.

This is another example of *low tolerance* and can often be addressed through *facilitation and support*.

An approach I have used successfully with insecure senior executives who fear embarrassment is to offer personal coaching in the new skill, without others knowing. The protégé can then emerge as competent and confident, leading change rather than passively following.

In summary, don't let anyone lose face.

6 *A senior member fears they will lose status, involvement, influence or control.*

Many long-serving Freemasons have built a particular reputation, status and sense of self-esteem on the back of their long service to their Lodge(s). That self-esteem or status may rest upon their knowledge or central involvement in Lodge matters, or from being a controlling or influential person in major decisions.

This is an example of *parochial self-interest*, the first type of resistance, and it may involve emotional elements shrouded in rational argument. Change often increases the involvement and influence of those who are skilled in what is being introduced, while compelling others who have held positions of influence to retire.

A solution is to encourage the member or members to *participate* in the change process. Reassure them that change will only happen after discussion, that anything new would be tried, tested and checked before the change is implemented and that their wise counsel would be sought all the way through the process. Continued *involvement* respectful of their position may secure their support for the change process.

Some brethren may also need *facilitation and support* to help them think through the need for and approach to change. However, this may need to come from a peer, or someone perceived as more senior.

An experimental change that proved to be beneficial and successful is unlikely to be reversed by even the most resistant of members, especially if they are seen to be part of the change.

In summary, consult and involve the key influencers and respect their position.

In all of the above, your best tools will be shared goals, patience and a determination to do what brethren agree is right for the Lodge.

However, you may still find yourself confronting a fundamental question. If – despite all your best efforts – a minority of members continue to resist a change that the majority wish to introduce, how far are you prepared to go to secure their support? Will you delay the change, despite the will of the majority, in order to maintain the support of the few? If so, for how long? And at what cost to the Lodge?

At what point will you decide that the good of the Lodge and the will of the majority must prevail, even at the cost of losing valued, possibly longer serving, members?

If you and your Lodge do have to confront this decision, I encourage you to take into account the needs and concerns of all members and have your eye on the future of the Lodge as well as its past. Regrettably, I have seen Lodges give in to overbearing senior members who use their status to obstruct change. The outcome, inevitably, is a decline in the Lodge and, in some cases, its demise and closure.

In conclusion

Not everyone resists change but those who do tend to have a concern or fear about losing something. Understanding those concerns and fears, and the way they manifest in a member's action, is key to deciding how to respond to and address that resistance. We can use approaches to change developed in other organisations, together with an understanding of Freemasonry's principles and culture, to develop responses to resistance and to implement change in a way that carries members forward together.

---

[1] See for example Carl Jung's rational functions as described in
https://www.businessballs.com/self-awareness/personality-theories-and-types/
[2] John P. Kotter & Leonard A. Schlesinger (1979) 'Choosing strategies for change', Harvard Business Review, 57, 2, pp. 106–114.
[3] Described in Kurt Lewin's Force Field Analysis model. See for example
https://mindtools.com/pages/article/newTED_06.htm
[4] Described in the Kubler-Ross Change Curve. See for example

   https://www.cleverism.com/understanding-kubler-ross-change-curve/

5 Kotter, J.P. & Schlesinger, L. A (1979) again.

6 These are two of the four stages of learning, first identified by Martin Broadwell and W. Lewis Robinson. See https://www.businessballs.com/self-awareness/conscious-competence-learning-model/

Chapter 8

Communication is Everything

When I get to know a new business client, I arrange to speak to a cross section of staff and employees. I ask them to list three issues that need attention in the organisation. In over thirty years of doing this, communication has always featured in everyone's top three.

This is not necessarily because the organisation or its staff or employees are poor at communicating. It is because our own expectations of communication can never be an exact match to those of anyone else. What we want from a communication is not easily understood or satisfied by the other party or parties.

We almost always want different information or participation than what we are offered. Or we want it in a different format, over a different channel or at a different rate.

This mismatch creates disappointment, frustration, confusion – or worse.

Lodges, and Freemasonry as a whole, are no different in this respect from other organisations. We as Freemasons are no different from the staff, employees, or customers in other organisations. We have expectations of information and communication that are rarely fully satisfied.

To explain why I think this is, I shall break the communication process down into its component parts. I will examine each of those parts. I will then use these to build a simple approach to communication that we can use in our Lodges.

However, first I am going to outline a typical Lodge scenario and consider why communication is often not as effective as it could be.

Two weeks in advance of a Lodge bar-b-que, organised to attract friends to the Lodge, the Secretary sent a booking form to all members as an attachment to an email. The subject line of the email included the event title but not the date. The email provided detailed instructions for booking to attending the bar-b-que. One of the instructions was to send the booking to the Assistant Secretary, with payment in advance, as the Secretary would be away on holiday. At the end of these details, the Secretary also asked, in the same email, for members to volunteer to deliver parts of the ceremony for an upcoming Lodge meeting.

In advance of the bar-b-que, the Secretary's email account received several bookings but they did not know about them until they returned home from holiday the day before the bar-b-que. They alerted the Assistant

Secretary who made last minute arrangements to increase the amount of food available, paying for this out of their own pocket.

After the bar-b-que, several members expressed disappointment at the low numbers attending, and the fact that no friends or guests of members were present. Others said they had not received the details and others still said they didn't know the date. At this point, no one had volunteered to deliver parts of the ceremony.

The Secretary pointed out that the email was sent "a full two weeks in advance of the bar-b-que", and that it included full booking details and the request for volunteers. They reminded members that the date for the bar-b-que had been agreed at the last committee meeting, some months previously. The Secretary believed they had communicated with the members but that too many of them lacked interest and didn't support them or the Lodge. Matters got quite heated, so the Master decided to phone the twenty-four members of the Lodge. The Master's findings were:

- Five did not recall receiving the email. Two of these subsequently found the email in their spam folder.
- Four said they saw the email but were not interested in the bar-b-que so did not open it.
- Three said they had seen the email and left it in their inbox to deal with later, not realising the date was so imminent.
- Four opened the email and read as far as the date. As they had already booked for other commitments, they did not attend. They did not read the email any further.
- Two members opened the email but did not act immediately. They could not find the booking form when, at a later point, they wanted to book to attend.
- Six members booked for and attended the bar-b-que, with their family. None brought any guests. One explained it was too short notice to bring anyone else.

Let us now break down the communication issues involved in this scenario.

1 *Sending is not the same as receiving.*

Just because a message has been sent, it does not mean it has been received. All communication processes run the risk of obstruction between sending and receiving. Sometimes this is due to the method of communication, or "communication channel" (in this case email), failing. Sometimes it is due to the intended recipient not attending to the channel. For example, some don't open their email system very often. Sometimes the intended recipients filter the information coming to them over a particular communication channel. They receive the communication but don't open or attend to it.

2 *Receiving is not the same as processing.*

Just because a message has been received, it does not mean it has been fully processed. In the above scenario, some opened the email but did not read all its contents. This often happens when the communication holds little interest, or perceived relevance or importance, for the recipient.

3 *Processing is not the same as understanding.*

Just because recipients process the contents of a communication, it does not mean they understand what the sender intended. In the bar-b-que scenario those who booked via the Secretary had misinterpreted the booking instructions.

Sometimes the language used by the sender is a barrier to a recipient understanding what was intended. Clearly, if the recipient does not understand the sender's language or dialect, they will not understand the message. However, language here can also refer to vocabulary and language style. Vocabulary is the range and extent of words we use. Somebody with limited vocabulary can be said to have a young reading age and requires information to be presented in simple, every day, language using words with few syllables and short sentences. Language style can range from formal to slang, technical to everyday, or it can reflect a preference for language rich in visual, auditory, or tactile metaphors.

Ideally, the sender should use the language, vocabulary and language style preferred by the recipient(s).

4 *If the sender's intended message and the recipient's interpretation of that message are different, the communication has not been effective.*

The recipient's interpretation of a message is largely influenced by their past experience, their level of interest at the time, and their ability to process the language the sender used.

Most of us are familiar with Chinese whispers, where a message sent along a chain of people is distorted along the way so that the version (interpretation) stated by the last recipient is very different from that stated by the first sender. A great example of this is how the message, "*Send reinforcements, we are going to advance*", is distorted to become, "*Send three and fourpence, we are going to a dance*".

Asking a recipient whether they understand a message cannot possibly provide any reassurance that they have. The only way to check understanding is to ask the recipient to repeat, or better still, explain the message.

5 *People prefer to receive, organise, and retrieve information in different ways.*

Some people like to receive information visually. They respond well to attractive promotional fliers. Others like information to be spelt out in short, clear sentences. Others like to be told things verbally. Some like to use technology, while others prefer not to.

Some people have very effective means of organising and filing information, whether that be using sophisticated memory techniques, in a structured physical filing system or organised in a hierarchy of folders on their computer hard drive. Others do little to organise information.

Some people are very good at retrieving information from memory. Others depend on their physical or computer filing system and develop elaborate search or indexing methods to help them do so.

As someone who has used computers all my working life, I save every document I receive – by email or elsewhere – in a designated folder on my computer hard drive. Until recently, I assumed most people did the same. I was quite shocked when I learned that many people leave email attachments in their email system and retrieve them by searching for the email.

6 *Structured communications are normally more effective than unstructured communications.*

Skilled communicators tend to use titles for their communications to attract interest and to help recipients filter relevant communications from the irrelevant. They also structure communications into introductions, the main body, and a summary. The introduction is used to, "Tell them what you are going to tell them." This allows recipients to prepare for a communication and create the means to organise the information. The main body is used to convey the information itself, ideally flowing in a meaningful way from one point to another and often with no more than a few key points. The summary is used to, "Tell them what you have told them". This technique is famously used by news programmes, starting with the headlines, and finishing with, "the main points of the news again".

The Secretary's email had a poor title. It did not refer to the date and so recipients could not filter its relevance and immediacy. It was also poorly structured and contained information (ie, about the upcoming ceremony) that was not relevant to the title and rest of the email, which was about the bar-b-que.

In addition to the communication issues described above, people vary in the management of their time. Some are very efficient and organised so act within other peoples' deadlines. Others have poor self-organisation and often miss deadlines. Lodge Secretaries soon learn which are which in their Lodge.

Having considered an example, I can now define successful communication. It is when both sender and recipient have the same understanding of a communicated message.

I have referred to communication channels. These are the methods a sender uses to carry a message to the recipient. Communication is most effective, or successful, when both sender and recipient are aware which channels are being used, monitor them regularly and engage with the other when a message is received.

Communication channels can be categorised in different ways. One distinction is between synchronous and asynchronous channels. Another is between digital and print.

"Synchronous communication" occurs when all parties are communicating at the same time, even if they are not in the same place. While face to face in the same room might be optimum, phone calls and – nowadays – video-conferencing are also very good alternatives for some purposes.

Written communications, such as printed materials and email, are examples of "asynchronous communication". These occur when people are not attending to a communication at the same time.

Traditionally, Lodge Secretaries used post ("snail mail") as the channel for formal, asynchronous, communications and the phone for more immediate, synchronous, communications. Nowadays the default communication channel used by most Secretaries is email. The ease and widespread use of email has led to a proliferation of communications and – sometimes – a loss in clarity. However, some members still don't use email and others don't consult it very often. There is growing evidence that younger people prefer not to use email.

However, email is only one example of written digital channels. Other examples include websites and social media, such as Facebook, Twitter, WhatsApp, and Instagram. All of these allow the sender to upload images and documents. Social media is especially useful as an immediate, dynamic, informal communication channel.

Audio and video digital channels include asynchronous examples such as podcasts and YouTube, and synchronous examples include video-conferencing platforms, such as Zoom.

As well as digital channels, there are the more traditional (and asynchronous) approaches of print media, such as books, newsletters, leaflets, posters, and brochures.

All senders have preferred channels for sending communications and all recipients have preferred channels for receiving them. If a sender wishes to ensure a message is received, processed, and interpreted accurately, the best method is to use the channel or channels preferred by the intended recipients.

One approach to understanding and improving our communication is known as the systems approach. It looks at all elements in communication as being part of a system and suggests how we can use these elements to good effect.

According to the systems approach,[1] the key elements in communication are the following:

1. The parties in the communication, namely the sender and recipient or recipients.
2. The sender's communication objective, or what the sender wants the recipient(s) to do as a result of the communication.
3. The message, or the core information that the sender wants the recipient(s) to receive, interpret and act upon.
4. The language used in the message, including technical versus everyday vocabulary and language style.
5. The amount of information in the message, and whether it is broken up into chunks which are more easily received, processed, and interpreted.
6. The structure of the communication, including an introduction which prepares recipients for what is to follow, the information itself under key points or headings, and a summary to remind recipients of the key points.
7. The channel to be used by the sender and recipient(s), and whether the channel is free from obstruction or distortion (ie, what is known as noise).
8. Whether there is a natural and easy connection (ie, rapport) between sender and recipient.
9. Whether the sender has the recipient's attention, or not.
10. Sending the information in chunks and waiting for the recipient(s) to acknowledge each chunk.
11. Asking the recipient(s) to confirm receipt and their interpretation of the message.
12. Including a "call to action", such as making a booking.
13. Responding to the recipient(s) interpretation of the message, clarifying any inaccuracies.
14. Closing the communication.
15. Following up any actions required by, or agreed in, the communication.

Using the above will help you to improve communication in any situation, not just in a Lodge.

Not all the above can be used in our email scenario, however. Email is asynchronous and, therefore, it is difficult to be sure that the sender and recipient are in rapport, have each other's attention and can send, receive, and acknowledge a message in chunks. Often the sender and recipient end up exchanging lengthy emails.

The systems approach is most effective when we are using synchronous communication. We have to work much harder to get our message across using asynchronous methods.

If we want to increase the number of responses we get from multiple recipients of a communication, there are several further techniques we can use, including:

- Issuing the same communication over multiple channels. These can be physical (printed), electronic (email, social media, websites) or face-to-face.
- Issuing the same communication, or similar, several times, starting much earlier before the critical deadlines. What may be missed on one occasion may be noticed on another. In addition, familiarity builds awareness, which must precede action.

Product marketing experts rely on these techniques to build successful advertising campaigns. We are seeing increasing use of advertising and marketing techniques by successful Lodges to promote their meetings to visitors as well as members.

Now let us build a new communication process to replace the single email that the Secretary used earlier.

1. The Lodge bar-b-que, its date, time, and venue, are included in an annual Lodge programme under "Social events".
2. The Secretary could go further and create an online calendar for the Lodge, covering all planned events and with access for all members and "friends" (regular visitors) of the Lodge.
3. Consider the different audiences for the communication (eg, Lodge members, regular visitors, the Province or District) and the

language style they prefer. If an audience includes those who are not Freemasons, avoid using the language of the ritual.

4. Identify the communication channels the audience members prefer to use and make sure communications are sent across these channels. These might include email, post, WhatsApp, Facebook groups, etc.
5. Schedule a sequence of communications over an extended time period, so that the message becomes familiar.
6. Draft the message, breaking it up into easily absorbed "chunks". Use short, simple, sentences and bullet points. Repeat any deadlines. Write a compelling title with sufficient detail to ensure it is attended to in time. Add an introduction, a summary, and a call to action.
7. Use separate communications for separate events, so that they can be easily searched and found.
8. Instead of creating booking forms as email attachments, use online booking forms. Both Google and Microsoft offer easy to create and easy to access online forms. These have the benefit of saving time by collating all respondent information at one time in one place, into a downloadable spreadsheet.
9. If payment is being collected at time of booking, use an online booking system such as Eventbrite. An Eventbrite account can be connected to the Lodge bank account so that payments go directly into Lodge funds.
10. Make use of booking acknowledgements (available in online forms) to summarise the information entered by the recipient. This can be easily printed out and for use on the day of the event.
11. Monitor responses and issue additional reminders before the deadline if required.
12. If response rates are low, use additional channels, including the telephone for any who do not respond as or when you would expect.
13. Send a final communication to the audience after the deadline to thank those who have booked and confirm bookings are now closed.

Much of the above process will be common to all Lodge events. It is quick and easy to set up and becomes easier with a little practice.

If we now look beyond Secretarial communications, happy and healthy Lodges are most likely to be fostered through open and inclusive communication between Lodge members. Different channels can be used, with social media – such as WhatsApp and Facebook – being very popular for informal "chat" within a closed group. Informal social events can complement the more formal Lodge meetings to build the bond between members, especially if Lodge meetings are infrequent. Some Lodges are now replacing Lodge committees with open forums, to discuss matters of interest. When committees or forums are held, remote members can be involved using video-conferencing, such as Zoom. All of these can help develop a shared understanding within the Lodge, especially if members participate, offer ideas and listen to the views of others.

To summarise, communication is not simply the one way sending of information to recipients. It involves processing, interpretation, and action on the part of all parties. It is successful when all parties arrive at the same understanding of the communicated message. To achieve this result, we need to consider the audience and their preferences, the message, and the language to use, the multiple channels available and the frequency with which we will send the communication. The systems approach is a good way of considering all of these.

If I wanted to summarise this summary, I would simply say, "close the loop". As with successful planning, successful communication involves a loop. This time closing the loop involves confirming the intended recipients have received a message, understand what is intended and have taken the expected action.

I am sure communication will continue to be a challenge for all of us. However, applying the above techniques will reduce the difficulties and frustration and result in increased engagement by members.

---

[1] Based on Shannon & Weaver's systems model of communication. See Claude E. Shannon & Warren Weaver (1949), "The Mathematical Theory of Communication", University of Illinois Press

Chapter 9

Culture and Belonging

One of the big issues currently being discussed in many organisations is that organisation's "Culture".

Culture has been described as "The way we do things around here". It is intangible and yet very real. It reflects the patterns of behaviour widely adopted within that organisation. These patterns reflect beliefs, assumptions, informal rules, the way decisions are made and how the organisation functions in the outside world.

Some cultures are conducive to organisational health and success while some are less so. A Lodge is an organisation, and all Lodges have their own culture. As a member of several Lodges, I am very aware of how these cultures differ and the impact they have on their members.

It's my belief that Lodges should review their culture at regular intervals and, where necessary, adapt it to balance the needs of current, new, and future generations of members.

Those who study organisational culture have developed various models to describe culture and to assist with culture change. A basic understanding of the dimensions behind these models of culture will help with your review and development of your Lodge's culture.

Common to many models of culture is the distinction between visible and invisible elements. Visible elements are overt and available for all to see. They include the organisation's goals and purpose, patterns of dress (in our case, uniform and regalia), roles or offices, structures, symbols and artefacts (including images and, in our case, Lodge furniture). Invisible elements usually have to be absorbed and sensed. They include the organisation's shared values, assumptions, habits and traditions that are taken for granted and which normally go unchallenged.

Some models of culture concentrate on the degree of openness, feedback, and shared communication within the organisation.[2] For example, some organisations share information within their membership, encourage feedback and are open about ideas, opportunities, and performance. Others are very closed, keep key information to an inner circle and discourage anything that challenges the *status quo* and the discussion of new ideas.

Other models of culture consider the organisation's collective attitude towards risk and whether the organisation encourages members to take risks or not.[3] Strongly linked to risk is the organisation's attitude towards failure and blame. Does it penalise failure and apportion blame to individuals, or does it recognise failure as a by-product of experimentation, an opportunity to learn and improve. Risk averse and blame cultures tend to stifle ideas, creativity, and experimentation.

Two dimensions that form a very popular model of culture are external versus internal focus, and stability versus flexibility.[4] An external focused organisation is concerned with its purpose and direction within the wider world, and with its customers or potential members. An internally focused organisation is concerned with its employees or current members, their needs, views and wishes. A stable organisation tends to formalise processes and procedures and manages change through discussion and agreement. A flexible organisation is fast moving with few formal processes and an expectation that its members act on their initiative.

Central to many approaches to culture is an understanding of power and decision making. These consider where power and authority lie and whether they are held by one person, a select few or by all members. In some cases, there may be a formal structure suggesting that power is shared by all, but also an informal structure in which real power is held by one or two highly influential people. Many Lodges have the latter type of culture, although very few started in this way.

A closely related dimension to power is leadership style. A participative and consultative leadership style creates a very different culture to one in which decisions are made by one person, or a small sub-group, and imposed on the remaining members.

What is the relevance of these models and dimensions of culture to our Lodges and their future?

Studies of organisations place culture as one of the most important indicators of success and excellence.[5] Culture has a major influence on member satisfaction and enjoyment.

If you see your Lodge as existing for the benefit of its current members, then it is less likely to want to evolve or change its practices or culture. A consequence could be that the Lodge may be less attractive or satisfying to new members. Therefore, it may decline in membership and, eventually, close.

However, if you see your Lodge as existing to introduce new members into Freemasonry and to help those members get value from their membership, then it follows your Lodge ought to evolve over time to satisfy the changing needs of actual and potential members.

One way to evolve is to conduct a regular review of the Lodge, its practices, culture and "direction of travel".

A Lodge review should consider recent evidence of member and visitor satisfaction, including members' surveys and feedback from resignations. It should also involve open discussion and consideration of alternatives. In Chapter 10, "Planning in the Lodge", I outline how you can conduct a Lodge review.

If your Lodge wishes to review its culture specifically, you could ask all members to describe where they think the Lodge fits on the different dimensions I have listed, and where they would like it to fit. The following scales might be of help.

Openness and transparency:
Information limited to a small group　　　　　　Information shared openly with all
0 —— 1 —— 2 —— 3 —— 4 —— 5 —— 6 —— 7 —— 8 —— 9 —— 10

Attitude towards risk:
Averse to risk　　　　　　　　　　　　　　　　　　　Willing to experiment
0 —— 1 —— 2 —— 3 —— 4 —— 5 —— 6 —— 7 —— 8 —— 9 —— 10

Attitude towards failure:
Penalises failure, seeks to blame　　　　　　Learns from failure, avoids blame
0 —— 1 —— 2 —— 3 —— 4 —— 5 —— 6 —— 7 —— 8 —— 9 —— 10

External vs internal focus:
Focused on the wider world　　　　　　　　Focused on existing members
0 —— 1 —— 2 —— 3 —— 4 —— 5 —— 6 —— 7 —— 8 —— 9 —— 10

Stable vs flexible:
Formal change processes, slow to change　　Informal processes, encourages initiative
0 —— 1 —— 2 —— 3 —— 4 —— 5 —— 6 —— 7 —— 8 —— 9 —— 10

Power and authority:
Restricted to one or a few members　　　　　　　　Shared by all members
0 —— 1 —— 2 —— 3 —— 4 —— 5 —— 6 —— 7 —— 8 —— 9 —— 10

Leadership style:
Dictatorial   Participative and consultative
0 —— 1 —— 2 —— 3 —— 4 —— 5 —— 6 —— 7 —— 8 —— 9 —— 10

Once all the results are back from members, you can discuss the following at an open meeting:

1 How different members have different experiences of the Lodge and its culture
2 Whether there are differences in views expressed by the longer standing and newer members of the Lodge
3 What culture you would like the Lodge to adopt
4 What changes you can make to move the Lodge culture from its current situation to what you agree you would like it to adopt.

Based on my experience working in organisational change, helping organisations adjust to changing needs and expectations, as well my experience of membership organisations, including Lodges, I believe there is an overall approach you can consider when thinking about culture change in your Lodges.

First, you can conduct a Lodge review and identify those practices that members are happy and unhappy with, or those which they think will help or hinder the Lodge's future development.

Secondly, you can acknowledge and openly discuss the less visible and more informal aspects of Lodge culture, and in particular openness, information sharing, the distribution of power and decision making.

Thirdly, you can encourage increased participation and shared responsibility in Lodge matters, whether it be by sharing out tasks, activities, and roles or by encouraging new ideas and experimentation. Please remember, experiments don't always work but they often lead to better ideas.

Fourthly, I anticipate a need to balance external and internal focus. A lodge should exist for the benefit and Masonic education and enjoyment of its members. However, unless it has an eye to the outside and the future, it will not attract new members and will not be able to sustain itself.

Fifthly, while Freemasonry tends to communicate stability and enduring values, our Lodges also need a degree of flexibility if they are to accommodate 21st century lifestyles. The two are not incompatible. Stability of values and purpose can go hand in hand with flexible approaches to management, sharing work, involving people, and developing Masonic understanding. Increased flexibility will also reflect better tolerance and understanding of members and their circumstances.

Finally, the direction of travel for the power dimension is clearly towards it being shared among the members. Restricting power to a few long-serving members will not engage or satisfy the 21st century Freemason. This may be very difficult to accept for some members of an older generation. Many of them were brought up to recognise a hierarchy in authority and accepted that those more senior in experience or service tended to hold more power.

As I explain in Chapter 3, those in work today have a different experience of authority, are generally less deferential and judge people on their merit rather than their seniority. They also tend to expect that they will be treated based on their own merit, will be valued and respected and will be consulted and included. Therefore, they want their voice to be heard and consider their membership fee entitles this to be so. Satisfying these expectations is likely to increase their sense of belonging, engagement and commitment to the Lodge.

If your Lodge is to survive, and thrive, I suggest it reviews and – if it considers it necessary – changes its culture sooner rather than later. Not doing so will only delay one of two inevitable scenarios; either a later than optimum culture change as time replaces the longer serving with the newer members (if they still remain), or the demise of the Lodge as the longer serving refuse to adapt to the new reality.

I have much more to say about these matters in Chapter 6, "Who decides?", in Chapter 2, "We have NOT always done it this way", and in Chapter 7, "But they don't want to change".

---

[1] "For example, Herman's iceberg model (see Wendell L French and Cecil H Bell, Jr. (1978), "Organisational Development: Behavioural Science Interventions for Organisational Improvement", 2nd Ed, p16, Prentice-Hall) and Schein's levels of culture model (see Edgar H. Schein (1992), "Organizational Culture and Leadership", Jossey-Bass, San Francisco)."

[2] For example, Deal & Kennedy (see Terrence E. Deal & Allen A. Kennedy (2000), "The new corporate cultures: revitalising the workforce after downsizing, mergers and reengineering", Texere, London.)"
[3] Ibid.
[4] See Daniel R. Dennison (1990), "Corporate culture and organizational effectiveness", John Wiley & Sons, New York
[5] See Tom Peters and Robert Waterman (1982), "In search of excellence", Harper & Row, New York.

Chapter 10

Planning to Succeed

> *"Proper prior planning prevents poor performance."*
>
> *"Failing to prepare is preparing to fail."*
>
> Benjamin Franklin

If there is one central skill or technique that I consider to be absolutely essential, for the success and good management of any activity or concern, it is planning. Looking back, I realise that planning has permeated my whole life. Scouting taught me to *"Be prepared"*. My Teacher Training and Scout Leader training taught me to be goal orientated and how to plan systematically to achieve those goals. In all my experience in management and in voluntary organisations, good planning has contributed to my own and my teams' success.

Good things do not happen by chance. We cannot rely on experience or our wits to make a success of something. This is especially true in our Lodges. If we wish to succeed, we must plan ahead.

Most planning systems are built around what are called "planning loops". Typically, these involve a review of past experience, setting some goals, a plan of what you intend to do, taking actions and then another review. Then new goals are set, a new plan developed, and the loop continues. Therefore, planning is a continuous process, with the means built in to improve what we are doing with each new loop.

If anyone is in any doubt about the relevance of planning and management in a Lodge, let us remember that the role of the operative Master Mason was to plan the new structure and to supervise its building. Those of us charged with managing our speculative Lodges today clearly ought to plan.

In fact, I suggest we need three levels of plan in our Lodges. Or rather, we need to operate three connected planning loops at the same time. These are:

1. A long-term, three-to-five-year, Lodge Development Plan
2. An Annual Plan for the coming year
3. A Meeting Plan for each Lodge meeting or event.

Lodge Development Plan

The first of these planning loops, the Lodge Development Plan, is the subject of the Members' Pathway.[1] This offers a technique to review all aspects of a Lodge, including its focus, health, ritual, traditions, education, communication, social events, charitable activities, support for new members, care for members, governance and administration, and its expectations of members. You can use the technique offered in the Members' Pathway to create a tailored Lodge member questionnaire, and another one for regular visitors if you so wish.

The Members' Pathway then offers a method of Lodge planning to address issues identified in the review. Out of this will come a Lodge Development Plan, a succession plan of Lodge officers, and a Lodge and candidate profile or outline. A Lodge Development Plan should ideally cover a period of three to five years. What you agree in the plan will also feed into any promotional materials you develop, including a website and social media.

I would recommend all Lodges to work through the Plan stage of the Members' Pathway at regular intervals of, say, every two to three years. This will keep the development plan fresh and relevant, and the Lodge focused on the future and alert to the changing needs of its members.

The Lodge Development Plan should drive all subsidiary plans. Use it as a reference, or start point, for every annual plan. Discuss it at Lodge committee meetings and refer to it on all other occasions when you are considering other plans. It should be a live document, used to inform other activities.

The Lodge Development Plan will also include your expected timings or deadlines for certain things to happen over the course of a few years. These should be updated and adjusted as annual plans progress, as they succeed or possibly fall short.

Annual Plan

The second planning loop is concerned with the annual Lodge cycle that begins with the Installation of a new Master. However, the work to plan for the year does not begin at the Installation. As a Lodge Secretary I used to meet with the anticipated Master of the following year around ten months before they were due to be Installed. At the first meeting we would discuss the role of the Master. Primarily, this is to preside over the Lodge, give it leadership, and leave it in a better position than when they found it. I would end that meeting by asking them to go away and think of what they would like the Lodge to achieve during their year as Master. I would ask them to consider:

1. Aspects of the Lodges development plan that are due to be actioned or delivered during their year
2. The Lodge succession plan, officers, and emerging talent
3. Ceremonies, ritual, and the wide involvement of members
4. Candidates / new members
5. Charitable goals
6. Social events.

At a follow up meeting a couple of weeks later we would discuss these goals – as that is exactly what they were – and formulate a draft plan for their year. Over the coming months we would involve other officers in the development of the plan. By the time of the Installation, the plan was well developed. The newly Installed Master would use it to provide an inspiring overview at their Installation Festive Board, thus fulfilling a primary leadership function of articulating and promoting a vision of the future.

Throughout their year in the chair, the Master and their various officers can then use the annual plan as the basis or start point for more specific plans for each meeting or event. They can also feed their experiences of success, or otherwise, into the next discussion of the Lodge Development Plan

Meeting or Event Plan

Planning for each meeting and event starts by referring to the annual plan. This makes sure that what was included in the annual plan for the particular event is then carried into the event plan itself. This, more detailed, meeting or event plan can be built around a running order, with clear timings and responsibilities defined.

As a Secretary, I produce an "extended agenda" with the Master and Director of Ceremonies. It follows the agenda in the summons convening the Lodge but expands on all the further detail required. For newly Installed Masters it spells out all the things they need to do that are not detailed in the ritual. It also identifies everyone who has a speaking part within the meeting.

For Lodge meetings, this approach saves "transition time" in the Lodge and at the Festive Board. By transition time I mean time spent asking others, or waiting for others, to do something. For example, there is no need to call on someone to propose the election of the Lodge auditors if the two people assigned to do this in the meeting plan simply stand and briefly say their piece. When everyone knows in advance what they are asked to do, and when, the non-productive transition time is drastically reduced.

Planning each meeting in detail is a major contributor to providing a great experience for all members, and particularly those who are new and still getting used to Freemasonry. Today's working members, especially, are used to being consumers and customers of services. They expect their "buying experiences" to deliver high quality. Thoroughly planning a meeting helps to achieve the first two of the "Seven habits of highly successful Lodges"; 1) great ritual and ceremonial and 2) good management.

After every meeting and event, a brief review involving the key players will feed back into the annual plan those things that went well, those things that did not and any things which still need to be addressed or improved upon in future.

How to prepare Lodge Development Plans

A straightforward and very effective approach to preparing these is to use the Success Cycle.[2]

The Success Cycle is an approach I developed in my professional work as a leadership and management coach, supporting and developing people and their organisations. It aligns a long-term aspirational view of what we wish our future to be like with our day-to-day actions and use of resources. It was inspired by a quote from Joel Barker, who said:

> *"Vision without action is merely a dream.*
> *Action without vision just passes the time.*
> *Vision with action can change the world."*

The Success Cycle provides the means for our long-term vision, hopes and dreams to drive and direct our day-to-day actions and for us to keep those day-to-day-actions focused on achieving the vision. It prevents us from losing our sense of purpose.

It does this by creating a six-step planning loop that "joins up the dots" between vision and action.

Diagram 1

In the following, I will explain how to use the Success Cycle, together with the Members' Pathway, to complete a fundamental review of the Lodge and create a Lodge Development Plan. Then I will look at how we can adapt the approach for an Annual Plan.

Review and learning

For a Lodge, as in any functioning organisation, the real start point for future planning (and for the Success Cycle) is a review. The review technique detailed in the Plan element of the Members' Pathway is ideal for an initial Success Cycle review. It should be a consultative process, drawing on the views and opinions of all members of the Lodge.

The consultation is best carried out using an initial survey or questionnaire, followed by discussion groups. I would recommend not using formal committees for this purpose but a more open and inclusive approach, possibly led or facilitated by the Lodge Membership Officer, by another experienced member with the appropriate skills or by a member of the Provincial Membership Officer's team.

The output from the review will be a series of conclusions and ideas which will influence the Lodge's vision for the next few years. Defining the vision is the next step in formulating the Lodge Development Plan.

Defining your Lodge vision

A vision is a clear, ambitious, and compelling view of what you would like your Lodge's future to be at a fixed point in the future. It is a dream; something positive and aspirational to be imagined. It acts as a compass point, giving a purpose and direction, and as a criterion against which your plans, decisions, actions and use of time, money and other resources can all be compared.

A good vision is focused on a point in the future beyond which you do not normally think, plan, or even imagine. This horizon is not so far away as to be out of sight and easily forgotten but also not so close that it gets mixed up with your day-to-day concerns. It must be visible (in your imagination) but currently out of reach.

By imagining a point some way into the future, you have time to build and carry out the plans necessary to turn your vision into reality. For many Lodges this is likely to be around five years from now, but it could be as little as three years or as many as seven.

Without such a vision your Lodge will have no compass point, no direction, no basis for goal setting or planning and no real direction or purpose.

"If you don't know where you are going, any road will take you there."
George Harrison

A vision can be thought of as a big or overarching goal. However, a vision does not comply with the normal rules for setting goals. You do not have to know – yet – how you will achieve it. Nor do you need to apply any "measures of success". All these things will come at later points in The Success Cycle.

A Lodge vision ought to be developed and agreed with others, ideally by following a Lodge review. Any group that agrees a shared vision is on its way to becoming a team. Working together towards that vision will strengthen the Lodge and keep it focussed. Successful leaders promote and sell a shared vision of future success and use it to inspire others and to engage them in an enterprise.

A vision will prompt the Lodge to plan in the longer-term rather short-term. It will require your dedication and the commitment of resources. However, a vision also requires a degree of flexibility. Your circumstances will change while you are working towards your vision, and you will need to be able to adapt.

A good vision is expressed in the present tense and in very positive and aspirational language. This will help you to imagine the vision as being true, or at least possible.

Imagination is important. If your Lodge members can imagine your vision being true the vision will be more compelling, powerful, persuasive, and irresistible.

A good vision should be easy to communicate and easy to remember. Your vision should not be too long. It should be just long enough to be clear and relatively specific. If it is too long it takes too much effort to learn and can be easily forgotten. A long vision is also more likely to become too specific and too limiting or restrictive as circumstances evolve over time. Equally, a vision is not a marketing slogan or strap line. It should not be so brief as to lack any context or meaning or clarity.

Just thinking of the vision should help you to imagine your success at achieving it. For example, *"To be the best Lodge"* is unlikely to trigger your imagination in any of your senses. However, the following may well do so:

"Our vision for Our Lodge No. NNN is to be an attractive, nurturing, supportive and growing Lodge offering a great experience of Freemasonry for all with an interest in XXX."

Note that this example also refers to members having a shared interest. It is helpful if the vision defines the people you wish to target as future members, whether they all share the same hobby (eg, motorcycling, Scouting, historic re-enactment) or background (eg, former pupils of a particular school) or profession (eg, leadership coaches!).

Visions differ from missions. A mission defines what an organisation is currently seeking to achieve. Its language is likely to be more practical or mechanical than the aspirational language of a vision.

My favourite means to distinguish between a vision and a mission is to use Admiral Nelson's examples. His vision was, *"England free from the threat of attack"*. His mission – which existed to make the vision come true – was, *"To annihilate the enemy"*.

Here are some past and present examples of organisational visions. All the following organisations are considerably larger than a Lodge. However, they are organisations that you will know and recognise so you may well see how their visions translate into, or drive, their collective actions.

> *"Our vision is to be earth's most customer centric company; to build a place where people can come to find and discover anything they might want to buy online."*
> Amazon.com

> *"A just world, without poverty."*
> Oxfam

> *"We seek to save a planet, a world of life. Reconciling the needs of human beings and the needs of others that share the Earth."*
> WWF

> *"To make people happy."*
> Disney

> *"To organize the world's information and make it universally accessible and useful."*
> Google

One way to create a Lodge vision is to ask members to imagine they stepped into a time machine, set the dials for a date exactly three or five years in the future, pressed the button, shot forward in time, and then got out. A Lodge vision defines exactly what you would all like to see, hear or experience the Lodge being, or doing, once you stepped out of the time machine. It should be aspirational, something positive and attractive.

Once everyone has done this, collate all the individual visions and look for themes. Cluster "like with like" without changing any of the wording, to identify similarities and differences. Discuss these openly, to arrive at a consensus of opinion before attempting to summarise this as a vision statement. It would be a mistake to try to craft the actual or final words before understanding the sentiments. Achieving consensus normally requires some, possibly all, members to sacrifice some of what they ideally want to arrive a point at which everyone can agree. However, it should not be too simplistic or generic as to apply to any Lodge.

Clarifying your Lodge's values

Closely allied to an organisation's vision are its values. Values represent what the organisation and its members hold to be important to them. Values help define an organisation's culture. When people share the same values, they are more likely to work together to achieve the same goals. When their values differ, they are more likely to work in opposition to each other.

Freemasonry has well developed and defined values, and we hope that these will help unite a Lodge in its vision and purpose. The language we use to express these within our ritual are:

Brotherly love
Relief
Truth

In the public domain we use the more widely understood words:

Integrity
Friendship
Respect
Charity

A Lodge could define additional values, specific to the Lodge and the way it functions. If it does so, it might want to keep these to just one or two, so as not to create too long a list.

A vision and values have the strongest impact when they act as a foundation stone, or reference point, so that they underpin all the Lodge's activities, especially all its dealings with people – whether members, families, guests, and candidates.

Setting your Lodge's goals

Once you have a clear vision of what you ultimately wish your Lodge to become in the long-term, you can create some shorter term "stepping-stones". These provide a route to take you step-by-step from where you are now – as represented by your Lodge review – to where you want to be at a point in the future – as represented by your Lodge vision.

To create such "stepping-stones" we now turn to goals. A lot has been written on goal setting. Here I will outline a simple approach that I have found more successful than most.

You can think of goals as things we set out to achieve at future points in time. We can create a series of connected goals to be achieved over time. Each goal will build on those previously achieved and each will take us closer towards our vision. Goals structured like this enable us to achieve our ambitious vision by following a series of shorter, more achievable but connected, steps.

It is best to involve several people in drafting goals. Then, once you have drafted them, you can confirm them with all members of the Lodge. This will create a sense of ownership of, and commitment to, the goals. This will help when you wish to refer to them as your plans progress.

To use goals in this way, we first break the vision down into a sequence of steps (our "stepping-stones") or smaller achievements. Each step follows those that have gone before and takes you to the next within a given period. This ensures you move towards achieving your vision at a rate that you can manage. The key is to set the steps the right distance apart, at the right intervals. If they are too far apart, you will fail – and fall in the "water" between the stepping-stones! If they are too close together, you will spend a lot of effort without getting very far.

Each area of Lodge activity addressed in your plan should have a goal at each stepping-stone. By area, I mean issues such as "ceremonial", "social", "membership", "committee", etc. Each area should also have something you can use to measure your progress. Let us call this a "success indicator". It might be a statistic, or it might be an achievement. The following are examples:

Membership:	Five-year net growth (see Chapter 2)
Progression:	Only Master Masons installed as WM
Social:	Growth in members and visitor attendance
Ceremonial:	Participation by Light Blue members

Good success indicators measure success, rather than failure. They have the effect of lifting spirits.

By setting a goal for each area using a success indicator you can ensure you make progress at each milestone.

Many people set goals using the SMART technique. I am not a fan of the original and most widely known version of SMART, which I believe encourages lack lustre development, so I will not repeat it here. Instead, I have produced my own, which I believe produces better results. In my version, SMART stands for:

1. Stretching (goals should not be too easy, nor too difficult).
2. Monitored (we should be able to track progress towards the goals using undisputed and easily available data).
3. Aspirational (goals should inspire us to be better than we are at present).
4. Relevant (goals should reflect our purpose and priorities).

5 Time limited (we should have a clear and unequivocal deadline for each goal to be achieved).

Each goal should meet the above SMART criteria and should define an achievement, outcome, or result, rather than an intention or activity. The following are examples of SMART goals:

By the Installation meeting in 20YY, we will have:
1 Created an ideal candidate profile (see the Members' Pathway).
2 Introduced at least NN new Initiates and MM joining members.
3 Retained all existing members, with no avoidable losses.
4 Identified the needs, interests, and wishes of all members of the Lodge relating to their participation and involvement in the Lodge and its activities.
5 Offered every member an opportunity to contribute to the activities of the Lodge appropriate to their interests and wishes.
6 Created a rolling Lodge succession plan.
7 Introduced meaningful education about Freemasonry as a regular part of the Lodge programme.
8 Organised and run an annual programme of social activities to satisfy the different interests of members and their families.
9 Appointed a Lodge communication officer and produced a communication plan, including social media.
10 Reviewed, agreed, and updated the Lodge Development Plan (see the Members' Pathway).

The above goals all start with a deadline, the Installation meeting of the year 20YY. They are also written in the past tense, so they define what will have been achieved by that deadline.

By setting goals over a series of consecutive deadlines, goals provide the stepping-stones towards the vision. Each goal is stretching in its own right but not so stretching as to be impossible. In this way, the achievement of each goal takes us closer to achieving a vision which, when originally set, may have appeared unrealistic.

For a three-to-seven-year Lodge Development Plan, I suggest you set goal deadlines – your stepping-stones – at six-month intervals. This will allow you to link your Lodge Development Plan to each Annual Plan. Each Master will preside over two reviews of the Lodge Development Plan, increasing the chance that progress will be made. This approach will also ensure that each Annual Plan makes a positive contribution to the achievement of the Lodge Development Plan.

The range of goals should cover all aspects of the Lodge's life and activities. The Lodge review process in the Members' Pathway is comprehensive in its scope and the goals should also cover the same breadth. Defining goals in this way will ensure that all aspects of the Lodged develop at the same time.

Building the plan

The first two steps in the Success Cycle, vision and goals, are leadership activities. They are concerned with future direction. The next three steps – starting with planning – are about management. We are now concerned with using time, skills, and other resources, to make things happen to achieve your goals.

Moving to the next step in the Success Cycle, planning, we now turn our attention to how you will achieve your vision and goals. Within the Success Cycle, the plan does a simple but essential job. It tells you, "Who will do what by when".

As we are now concerned with management, it is likely that those Lodge officers with management roles will do much of the detailed planning. These include the Secretary, Director of Ceremonies, Almoner, Charity Steward, Membership Officer and Mentor.

Plans tend to be logical and structured. They map out a sequence of activities and the resources required to carry out the activities. Many plans are documented using tables such as the following:

Goal	Activities (What)	Responsible (By whom)	Resources (How much)	Deadline (By when)	Success indicator	Current status
1.						
2.						
3.						
4.						
5.						

Table 4

This approach provides a direct link between your goals and the details of your plan. For example:

Goal	Activities (What)	Responsible (By whom)	Resources (How much)	Deadline (By when)	Success indicator	Current status
Organised and run an annual programme of social activities to satisfy the different interests of members and their families.	Review previous social events. Identify issues and links from Lodge vision. Ask the next WM for their wishes. Survey members interests / wishes. Create options. Plan implementation. Review progress.	Lodge social committee (for planning the programme). Organisers for each event. Others to support the organisers.	Entertainers / attractions. Venues. Contacts. Budget.	Election meeting each year.	Attendance by • Members • Families • Guests • Potential members Favourable feedback.	

Table 5

This also shows that you can have different levels of detail within a plan. The above is part of a Lodge Development Plan and provides a high-level framework for planning the annual social programme. It does not cover the detailed planning for each event within that programme. At the time you define the high-level plan (ie, that above) the details for each year, let alone each event, cannot be known. Therefore, the team will develop more detailed, subordinate, event plans to deal with the finer details.

Despite the structured and logical nature of plans, and the planning process, I have found that the best plans are developed after a period of creative thinking. This involves one or more people first generating and considering lots of options. They then select from several alternatives those activities best likely to achieve the goals.

While producing a plan, you might also consider how you will track or monitor the progress and delivery of the plan. This is covered in step five in the Success Cycle, and is explained below. However, it may be easier to think about this now, so that you can decide what information you will want to use to check that your plan is on track.

When you have done this, you are ready for action!

Putting it into action

However well thought through your Lodge's vision, goals and plans may be, without action they will all come to nothing. However well intentioned, ambitious, and organised you and your Lodge may be, unless you act right then you will not arrive at your destination.

Having followed the process so far, you will understand that the actions you take must be aligned to your vision. This is what Joel Barker's quote is all about. The whole purpose of the intermediate steps, those between vision and action – the goals and plans – is to increase the likelihood that what you do and how you act at all times is consistent with that vision. Therefore, this Step answers the question, *"How do we spend our time and energy doing the right thing?"*

There are several things you can do to align your actions with your vision:

1. Keep the Lodge's vision clearly in mind, regularly. Refer to it often. Remind yourselves of why the vision is so important to you.
2. Imagine it as being true. Imagine the positive benefits for the Lodge and its members when it becomes true. What will it mean to you? What difference will it make to the Lodge? How will the Lodge be better?
3. Remind yourselves of your goals. Keep a written copy of your current goals in plain view in and around other Lodge materials. Recap them at regular intervals and refer to them often.
4. Remind Lodge members of the distance you have all travelled since you started your journey towards your vision.
5. Review your plans at regular and frequent intervals.
6. Establish new disciplines that put your vision and aligned actions into the forefront of your thinking. Practice these new disciplines until they become habits.
7. Refer to your vision and goals whenever discussing anything you are thinking of doing.
8. Consider all choices open to the Lodge and ask whether they are aligned to your vision. Select those options that are. Alignment is key.

Ultimately, the "right thing" is that decision or action which best aligns to, and moves you and the Lodge towards, your vision. Your goals and plans are subordinate to this vision. They serve your vision rather than replace it. Do not forget or abandon your vision as soon as you have your goals and plans. Keep your vision at the centre of your collective attention. If necessary, adapt your goals and plans, and ultimately your actions, to best suit the achievement of your vision.

Taking action requires judgement. You may find that you must make difficult choices. To overcome obstacles, you may have to deviate from what you had planned to do, and then adjust to get back on track. At all times, the criterion for what is "the right thing to do" is its alignment to the vision.

Any Lodge activity, or use of a resource, not aligned to the Lodge's vision is wasted, or at least misdirected. Therefore, it is very important to maintain attention and focus on the vision, goals, and plans. Lodge members' actions are most likely to be aligned to the vision if they all share the vision, commit to the goals, know the plan and act accordingly.

Values are also critical here. Our values drive our actions and behaviour. Aligning Lodge actions to our vision and values reduces inconsistency. It is also likely to contribute to increased harmony, happiness and satisfaction in the Lodge, and result in less anxiety, stress, and tension.

Monitor your progress

Monitoring your Lodge's progress is about checking that you and your members are doing what you said, in your plan, that you would do. Monitoring sits in the lower half of the Success Cycle. It is shorter term, regular and more mechanical. Simple tracking systems are very helpful here.

Many plans start out with good intentions. However, acting according to the plan requires more than good intentions; it takes discipline. Monitoring is a means to help you to sustain your Lodge's good intentions. You can think of it as your collective conscience. By monitoring your progress against your plan at regular intervals, you can:

1   Take remedial action if need be (to correct any deviation from plan).

2   Adapt the plan if a better means to achieve your goals becomes available.
3   Modify your use of resources if necessary or re-plan if you consider it appropriate.

The Lodge members, or at least the managers in the Lodge who devised the plan, should decide what you will monitor, and how you will do so. This is best done at the same time that you finalise your plan. It helps you put in place the means, or systems, you will use to capture data and monitor your progress. You can then take a "baseline" measure by capturing data at the start of your journey. You can refer to this baseline at regular intervals as your plan progresses, to measure your overall "distance travelled". Without a baseline, it is too easy to forget the magnitude of your progress or achievements. Without a baseline, your members and others are highly unlikely to appreciate fully what you have achieved.

To set up your monitoring system:

1   Decide what you will monitor. Include whether the Lodge has done what it said, in the plan, it would do. You can also monitor your "success indicators", as appropriate to your goals and plans. Examples might include, "5 year net growth", "Master Masons in office", "Visitor attendance", and so on.
2   Select a reliable source of data for each monitor. As far as is possible, the sources of data should be objective and easy to obtain at low cost and minimal effort. For example, "5 year net growth" can be calculated every year by the Lodge Membership Officer or Secretary (see Chapter 2).
3   Capture and record the data from that source at regular intervals. This is where the discipline comes in. A spreadsheet is a useful tool to record the data, especially if you summarise the data with metrics like average results.
4   Set up reminders to capture and log the data, especially in the early days before you have got into a habit of monitoring data or set up a procedure.
5   Share the data with Lodge members, to reinforce appropriate behaviours that are in everyone's control.

6   Put the data to good use by adjusting the plan, or its timescales or use of resources, to optimise your route to success.

Remember that your plan, and its monitoring system, is subordinate to your goals, which themselves are subordinate to your vision. If you decide to reformulate your plan, then you should then adapt your monitors to align them to the plan itself.

It is important to monitor and communicate success, and improvements towards success, so that people can learn from and be recognised or rewarded for it. Regrettably, many groups measure failure, resulting in a focus on underachievement. As "what you measure is what you get", a focus on failure can create a negative, complaining, and demoralising environment. In such circumstances many people hide their mistakes or blame others for them, rather than declare them, accept responsibility, and learn from them.

With a full set of monitors in place, you are ready to review your progress and achievements.

Reviewing and celebrating success

We now return to the top half of the Success Cycle, to the leadership activities.

Monitoring is a management activity to track whether you are keeping to your plan. Reviewing is a leadership activity that considers whether you are achieving your goals. Reviewing also helps you learn from past experiences and celebrate your success.

Reviewing is best done at the intervals set by your stepping-stones. So, for example, if you set goals to be achieved at six monthly intervals then you should hold a review at the same interval. Reviewing is not as mechanical as monitoring. It draws on the data obtained during the monitoring activities. It is best done by asking your members a series of questions. This could be done via an online survey, followed by an informal meeting.

The following are good examples of questions to ask.

- Have we achieved the goals we set ourselves to achieve by this date?
- What has gone especially well in that time?
- What difficulties have we had?
- What have we learned during that period?
- What can we do in the future to improve the Lodge plan?

If you hold a meeting to discuss these questions, I suggest you consider each question in detail and take note of every opinion, before arriving at general conclusions or consensus. It is not necessary for everyone to agree on each point, but it is important that every comment is considered. It is especially important that newer members are heard, and their views considered.

A review such as this will help you to refresh or improve your Lodge Development Plan. You may also want to adjust your goals, or perhaps their deadlines, as a result of the review.

One thing that often goes wrong with planning is that people lose track of progress. A lot of work may go into the plan and all its actions. However, unless your Lodge members are kept informed and involved, they may not relate what they experience to the plan itself. Therefore, it is important to keep referring to the plan, the goals and achievements, in regular oral and written communications.

At major intervals, when you have achieved something that you have planned, pause what you are doing and celebrate together.

A celebration is especially important at the end of the period covered by your Lodge Development Plan, even if you have not achieved everything you set out to do.

A celebration is a marker in time. It is something that creates great memories and allows everyone to share in their success. Celebrations come in all forms and might include, for example, special events, presentations, articles in newsletters, pages on websites, an entry in the Lodge history. What is important is that members feel that their hard work has been recognised and has been worth all the effort. Celebrations act as motivators to move on and continue the next set of plans and improvements.

Going round again

When you have reached the end of your development plan, and have celebrated whatever success you have achieved, you are ready to continue with the next loop in your Lodge Success Cycle. This involves:

1. Refreshing, updating, or creating a new Lodge vision – based upon the new situation of the Lodge.
2. Setting new or revised goals aligned to the refreshed, updated, or new Lodge vision.
3. Creating a new Lodge Development Plan, built around the new goals.
4. Putting in place new monitors to track the new plan.
5. Making sure all activities are aligned to the vision and fit within the plan.
6. Involving all members throughout the planning process, to get everyone's input and commitment.
7. Keeping everyone informed of progress.
8. Celebrating achievements.

How to prepare Lodge Annual Plans

A Lodge Annual Plan follows the same principles as a Lodge Development Plan. However, there are some key differences.

1 An Annual Plan is subordinate to the Lodge Development Plan
An Annual Plan should not deviate from what is contained within the Development Plan. It can add detail, but all elements should be aligned to and consistent with the bigger plan.

2 The vision and goals for an Annual Plan are defined by the incoming Master
The incoming Master's primary role is to preside over the Lodge and give it leadership. Setting a vision and goals for the year is a leadership act. Of course, the wise Master will consult others when devising them. They should also be aligned to,

and consistent with, the bigger Lodge vision and goals and they should help the Lodge achieve what has already been defined for the time period in the Lodge plan.

3 *Goals should be achievable within the Master's year*
The Master might set overall goals covering the whole year. Or they might set a series of milestone goals, to act like stepping-stones covering the whole year. In both cases the goals should not extend beyond their year as Master.

4 *It makes sense for the Master to involve others in planning how to achieve their goals*
Planning is a management role, and the Master should allow others to develop and implement the plans, so that they can concentrate on leadership.

5 *Review and celebration are just as important*
A review of an annual plan will allow the Master to reflect on their year and how they have contributed to the Lodge. It should also consider how their year has supported and contributed towards the Lodge development plan.

A good way to finish a Master's year is with a celebratory event prior to the installation of their successor. This allows the Lodge to recognise the contribution made by the Master without them overshadowing, or being overshadowed by, the Master Elect.

How to prepare for meetings and events

Planning and organising meetings and events is something with which most of us have some experience. They are also the simplest of the three levels of plans to prepare. Therefore, I will not cover them in very much detail. However, it worth examining how meeting or event plans can align with Lodge Development and Annual plans.

The start point ought to be the Annual Plan. In that you can list all the events you want during the year, whether formal meetings, social events, committees, and so on. Each event should have one or two goals that should align with the goals in the annual plan and contribute towards their achievement. Through the annual plan, they should also be consistent with and contribute to the overall development plan.

This alignment is what is known as the golden thread. It links all three levels of goals and plans together. The higher-level goals influence and provide boundaries for lower-level ones. By achieving lower-level goals the higher ones are one step nearer to being achieved. Having aligned goals also provides a framework for explaining to members what is happening and why.

I like using templates and checklists for plans. So, for example, I have a planning template for each regular meeting in the year, another for committee meetings and others for formal and informal social events. These templates list all the things that need doing, including a timeline for doing them, the people and other resources needed, to turn the plan into a successful event. They can be updated in the light of experience and review.

Another tip is to set up the plans using the templates early in the year. Then add detail as you get closer to the event, using the timeline to monitor progress and to set priorities.

Finally, as with all planning activities, make sure you review each event, even if informally in a discussion with other members or by asking them for feedback.

Summary

Good things do not happen by chance. They need good planning and organising. By planning at the three levels of Lodge development plan, annual plan, and event / meeting plan, you can be sure that all your activities are contributing to the overall and long-term success of the Lodge. It is essential to align these plans, to make sure their goals and actions are consistent and that everything that happens contributes to achieving your vision of the Lodge in the future.

[1] See https://b.ugle.org.uk/membership/members-pathway
[2] Tony Harvey (2018), "Introducing the Success Cycle: six steps to achieving your dream", Carrfields Publications.

To Summarise

In the following, I attempt to summarise what for me are the key messages from the previous chapters. There may, however, be other points that, for you, are equally important and relevant to you and your Lodge.

The seven habits of highly successful Lodges

Successful Lodges are strong, healthy and attractive to new and existing members. They have good prospects of continued viability.

By strong I mean they have members who are *able* and *willing* to take on all the various offices. By healthy I mean they have a continued supply of suitable candidates, a number of members who are developing in Freemasonry and a choice of people for the various offices. An attractive Lodge is one that draws people to it, that existing brethren want to visit, and potential members want to join. What sort of Lodge does that? One that promises and delivers an enjoyable experience that people want to repeat.

Lodges don't become or remain strong, healthy and attractive by chance. It takes effort far beyond organising one meeting to the next. It requires a continuous process of reviewing, planning and implementation.

Lodges can build their plans to excel in the seven-habits of highly successful Lodges, which are:

1. Great ritual and ceremonial
2. Good management
3. Active support for newer members
4. Engagement of all members
5. Distinctive features that evolve
6. Harmony
7. Leadership, energy and enthusiasm

These reflect the different aspects of Lodge life and ensure a balance between them; leadership vs management, ritual or meaning vs organisation, the needs and expectations of the individual vs those of the Lodge.

Chapter 1 sets out the seven habits in detail while later chapters provide rationales, explanations and techniques to manage the issues triggered by the habits themselves.

Membership myths and facts

Like all good plans, planning to become a highly successful Lodge really ought to start with an understanding of our past and present situations.

Analysis of historic membership data shows that in its first two hundred years Freemasonry experienced a steady growth. In the 20th century it experienced two tsunami effects, prompting significant and – as we have seen – unsustainable growth. Its current membership has returned to approximately the same as in 1920, but with twice as many Lodges and many more Masonic Halls.

Looking at current trends, we are losing just under 3,000 memberships each year. This is equivalent to a medium size Province closing every twelve months.

On average, every Lodge has admitted 11.6 Initiates in the last ten years. If a Lodge has retained all those members, it will be growing. The real challenge is to improve member retention, not find more members. The best way to do this is to fix the cause of the leak and stem the loss. Until we do this, admitting more new members to a declining Lodge is rather like continuing to pour water into a leaky bucket. However much effort we spend finding new candidates in such a situation is likely to be wasted as they are highly likely to leave.

Unfortunately, a quarter of our members report being less than happy with their membership. Such members are at risk of submitting their resignation. Their dissatisfaction is mostly due to not feeling valued or included, or to their expectations not being met. Where good quality care is given, and expectations are met, more members are retained.

New members' expectations of their Lodges are closely linked to their reasons for joining. Research has identified nine different reasons for becoming a Freemason. While Freemasonry can satisfy all nine of these reasons, no one Lodge is likely to be able to meet them all. We need more diversity between Lodges. This will create more options for potential members. It would help if more Lodges referred "poor fit" applicants to other Lodges, those better suited to their needs.

Most people (91%) join membership organisations after being approached by existing members or because of previous contact they have had with the organisation. Promotional activities directly generate only a minority of new members, just 9%. However, promotional activities do increase awareness, create a "positive public image", stimulate interest and make it easier for us to talk about Freemasonry.

Chapter 2 provides several sets of membership and related data. It also analyses the implications of this data for how we manage our Lodges and seek to grow our membership.

The world of the 21st Century Freemason

The lifestyle and work experiences of employees in the 21st century are very different to those of the late 20th century. There have been major changes in how organisations treat and involve their employees. This has impacted the mindset and expectations of those we are seeking to introduce into Freemasonry. They expect to be valued as individuals and respected and consulted as members. They expect to have a voice in anything that affects their membership and their development or progress. Their response to outdated approaches in Lodges that have not adjusted or evolved is likely to be negative. If Lodges wish to retain the 21st century Freemason, they ought to abandon the "conveyor belts" that so many have created, and which deliver "one size fits all" Freemasonry. Instead, I encourage them to adopt a more flexible "member centric" approach, developed around an understanding of each person.

Unless Lodges make these adjustments in their practices and cultures, unless they evolve to become better aligned to 21st century lifestyles and mindsets, they may find they will not retain enough of these outstanding people to ensure the continued existence of Freemasonry as we know it. In fact, if we don't make changes to our Lodge practices, the 21st century Freemason will eventually do so – when their time inevitably comes. So, we may as well start now.

Chapter 3 describes some of the major differences in the work experience and lifestyle of the 21st century Freemason and considers their implications for the management of our Lodges today.

We have NOT always done it this way

Charles Darwin observed that all populations change over time. His theory of natural selection explains why some groups within populations thrive while others fail. Essentially, small variations between those groups result in some of them being favoured over others in the struggle for limited resources. Darwin himself said there is, "One general law, leading to the advancement of all organic beings, namely: multiply, vary, let the strongest live and the weakest die". Perhaps a more familiar quote is by Megginson who said, "It is not the strongest that survive, nor the fittest, but those best suited to their environment and best able to manage change". Carl Sagan said, "Extinction is the rule. Survival is the exception".

If we apply these points to Freemasonry, then we should realise that Freemasonry is just one organisation a person might choose to join. Equally, they have plenty of Lodges to choose from. Each Lodge has to make its offer attractive to potential applicants. Each Lodge can introduce small variations to make itself distinctive in the hope that it will be favoured. Evolution also tells us that we cannot expect all our Lodges to survive; only those that are willing and able to adapt to their changing environments.

Organised Freemasonry has continually evolved over the course of its three-hundred-year history. The history of our oldest Lodges and the way in which they have adapted their practices give us an example to follow. Traditions also evolve, as the UK's oldest institutions – including the monarchy, City of London, the church and our oldest universities – demonstrate. Using tradition as a reason to prevent evolution and change is effectively granting voting rights to our predecessors and denying them to our current and future members. G.K. Chesterton called tradition the "democracy of the dead".

If we want our Lodges to thrive, we must allow them to evolve and we must manage the change process. Chapter 4 offers a change process for Lodges to follow.

Leadership and management in the Lodge

Leadership and management are different but complementary. Both are needed in a Lodge.

The Master's role is to provide leadership and direction during their term of office, leaving others to manage the delivery of plans. The managers are each responsible for an area of work and themselves lead teams. The Secretary manages Lodge administration, the Director of Ceremonies manages ceremonial, the Almoner or Mentor manages care and the Charity Steward manages fundraising.

Appointing appropriate people to appropriate roles is key and deserves careful forward planning. Finding people who are both able and willing to do a particular role is the secret to a Lodge's long-term success. A good approach is to discuss members' aspirations at regular intervals and build a succession plan that allows for a regular turnover of roles.

Good leaders concentrate on achieving tasks, supporting the group of people they work with and developing individuals. They adapt their "leadership style" to provide just the amount of direction and support that other members need. They also develop a team approach within the Lodge. A team approach to the management of the Lodge will help all officers and members do their tasks as well as is possible, for the benefit of all.

Chapter 5 describes several approaches to leadership and management that will help both the Master and their key officers be more successful.

Who decides?

The formal processes detailed in the Book of Constitutions provide a robust system for a Lodge to make decisions. However, in many cases Lodge committees, cliques and lone officers make decisions without fully consulting members or without building consensus. In the 21st century, members increasingly expect to be involved in Lodge decision making and to have their contributions heard and considered.

Including all members in Lodge decision making is likely to increase engagement. Consensus building is a helpful process which, along with the generation, consideration and evaluation of many different options, can result in increased buy-in and support for decisions. This helps promote the health and strength of the Lodge. However, committees have traditionally been exclusive and use majority voting, approaches that are not well suited to being inclusive and consensus building.

Chapter 6 expands on these points and includes a model for making decisions that will include all members in the steps involved, including creating ideas, reviewing them and reaching conclusions.

But they don't want to change

I often get asked, "What can we do about those members who resist any change? They are holding us back." Despite a common claim, it is not true that "no-one likes change." However, those who resist it tend to have a concern or fear about losing something.

Understanding those concerns and fears, and the way they manifest in a member's action, is key to deciding how to respond to, and address, that resistance. We can use approaches to change developed in other organisations, together with an understanding of Freemasonry's principles and culture, to develop responses to resistance and to implement change in a way that carries members forward together.

Chapter 7 includes an outline of various reasons for resistance to change, and some approaches that have proved to be successful at helping address resistance and building agreement to a plan for change.

Communication is everything

Regular communication to and between members acts as a glue within a Lodge. It builds a bond and encourages members to engage in activities and with each other.

Communication is successful when two or more people arrive at the same understanding of a message. Achieving this is not easy and certainly requires far more than simply sending information from sender to receiver, in one direction with no feedback.

It involves creating a connection between members and then processing, interpretation – and often action – on the part of all parties. To arrive at the same understanding of the communicated message, we need to consider the audience and their preferences, the message, and the language to use, the multiple methods of communication (or "channels") available, and the frequency with which we will send the communication.

Chapter 8 outlines several approaches Lodges can use to improve both formal and informal communication with and between members."

Culture and belonging

Culture has been described as "The way we do things around here". It is intangible and yet very real. It reflects the patterns of behaviour widely adopted within an organisation, in this case your Lodge.

Culture can be described using several different issues or dimensions, the main examples being described in chapter 9. Some Lodge cultures may have favoured past generations of members and might not be conducive to current or future generations. As part of the Lodge review process we can consider Lodge culture and make adaptations to suit the changing needs of current and future members, to increase the sense of belong, engagement and commitment.

Planning to succeed

Good things don't happen by chance. We cannot rely on experience or our wits to make a success of something. This is especially true in our Lodges. If we wish to succeed, we must plan ahead.

I suggest our Lodges should plan at three levels:

1. A long-term Lodge Development Plan
2. An Annual Plan for the coming year
3. A Meeting Plan for each Lodge meeting or event.

Good planning follows a loop. We start with a review, then set goals, decide what actions and resources will be the most appropriate to meet those goals, carry out those actions and finally review again before starting the next plan.

In chapter 10 I outline how my Success Cycle model and the Members' Pathway can be used together to create a Lodge development plan. I then look at how we can build an annual plan, aligned to the development plan and focused around the Master of the year and their hopes and aspirations. Finally, I suggest how each Lodge meeting and its festive board can be planned using an extended agenda or running order. This approach reduces "transition time" – the time spent between items on the agenda or between toasts at the festive board, when people are trying to figure out who is meant to be doing what.

Finally

I believe that the future of our Lodges will be secured if we create great experiences for new and existing members. However, we cannot rely on what worked in the past, our inherited customs and practices, to do this. Those people working in the 21st century have very different lifestyles to their predecessors and Lodges need to adapt to accommodate these changes.

All of this can be done without changing our purpose, values, landmarks or ritual. All of this can be done by following the example set by our growing and most healthy Lodges, by adopting the seven habits and by implementing the approaches and techniques outlined in this book.

Bibliography

John Adair (1973), "Action Centred Leadership", McGraw-Hill, New York.
Shainna Ali (2018), "What you need to know about the loneliness epidemic", Psychology Today.
Martin M. Broadwell (1969), "Teaching for Learning", The Gospel Guardian, Vol 20, pp 41-43.
Stephen Covey (1989), "The 7 Habits of Highly Effective People", Simon & Schuster, London.
James Daniel (2020), "Stuck with the Sussex fudge?", in Freemasonry Today, Winter 2020 edition, United Grand Lodge of England, London.
Charles Darwin (1859), "On the Origin of Species", John Murray.
DCMS (2019), "Community Life Survey 2018/19", Cabinet Office, London.
DCMS (2020), "Community Life Survey 2019/20", Cabinet Office, London.
Terrence E. Deal & Allen A. Kennedy (2000), "The new corporate cultures: revitalising the workforce after downsizing, mergers and reengineering", Texere, London.
Daniel R. Denison (1990), "Corporate culture and organizational effectiveness", John Wiley & Sons, New York.
Wendell L French and Cecil H Bell, Jr. (1978), "Organisational Development: Behavioural Science Interventions for Organisational Improvement", 2nd Ed, p16, Prentice-Hall.
Edward T. Hall (1976), "Beyond culture", Anchor Press, New York.

Tony Harvey (2012), "Scouting & Freemasonry: two parallel organisations?" (The 2012 Prestonian Lecture), Carrfields Publications.

Tony Harvey (2018), "The future of Freemasonry: evolution & change" (The 2018 Cornwallis Lecture), Kent Masonic Museum & Library Trust, Canterbury.

Tony Harvey (2018), "Introducing the Success Cycle: six steps to achieving your dreams", Carrfields Publications.

Rodney Hedley (1992), "Volunteering Today: facts and figures on volunteering in the UK for volunteer organisers", Volunteer Centre UK, Berkhamsted.

Stanley N. Harman in Wendell L French and Cecil H Bell, Jr. (1978), "Organisational Development: Behavioural Science Interventions for Organisational Improvement", 2nd Ed, p16, Prentice-Hall.

Paul Hersey & Ken Blanchard (1982), "Management and organisational behaviour: utilising human resources." Prentice-Hall, New Jersey.

Percy R. James (1967), "The Union and after, 1813-1917", in "Grand Lodge 1717-1967", UGLE.

Carl Jung (1971), "Psychological Types", Princeton University Press, New Jersey.

John P. Kotter & Leonard A. Schlesinger (1979) 'Choosing strategies for change', Harvard Business Review, 57, 2, pp. 106–114.

Elisabeth Kübler-Ross (1969), "On death and dying", Macmillan, New York.

Thomas S. Kuhn (1962), "The structure of scientific revolutions", University of Chicago Press.

John Lane (1895), "Masonic Records 1717-1894", 2nd Ed, Reprinted 2000, Lewis Masonic.

John Lane (1889), "A Handy Book to the Lists of Lodges", London.

Kurt Lewin (1947), "Frontiers in group dynamics: Concept, method and reality in social science; social equilibria and social change. Human Relations, Vol 1, pp 5-41.

Masonic Services Association of North America (2020), "US Masonic Membership Totals since 1924", See https://msana.com/services/u-s-membership-statistics/

Michael Lipka & Claire Gecewicz (2017), "More Americans now say

they're spiritual but not religious", Pew Research Center.
Natalie Low, Sarah Butt, Angela Ellis Paine & Justin Davis Smith, (2007). "Helping out: a national survey of volunteering and charitable giving", Cabinet Office, London.
Peter Lynn & Justin Davis Smith (1992), "The 1991 national survey of voluntary activity in the UK", Volunteer Centre UK, Berkhamsted.
Angel Millar (2019), "The future of Freemasonry: who we are and what we have to offer", The Plumbline, Vol 26, No. 4, Scottish Rite Research Society.
Tom Peters & Robert Waterman (1982), "In search of excellence", Harper & Row, New York.
Robert Putnam (2000), "Bowling Alone: the collapse and revival of American community", Simon & Schuster.
Graham Redman (2009), "Masonic Etiquette Today", Ian Allan Publishing.
Frederick F. Reichheld & W. Earl Sasser, Jr (1990), "Zero Defections: Quality Comes to Services", Harvard Business Review, Sept-Oct edition.
W. Lewis Robinson (1974), "Conscious Competency – The Mark of a Competent Instructor", The Personnel Journal, Vol 53, pp 538-539, Baltimore.
John Roscoe (2015), "Results from a survey of new Initiates in London", presentation for MetGL / MetGC.
John Roscoe (2015), "Results of the analysis of the second survey of Freemasons concerned with recruitment and involvement", Internal report for the UGLE.
Edgar H. Schein (1992), "Organizational Culture and Leadership", Jossey-Bass, San Francisco.
SIRC (2012), "The future of freemasonry: A report by the Social Issues Research Centre", UGLE, London.
Shalom H. Schwartz (1992), "Universals in the content and structure of values: Theory and empirical tests in 20 countries." In Mark P. Zanna (Ed), "Advances in experimental social psychology", Vol 25, pp 1-65, Academic Press, New York.
Claude E. Shannon & Warren Weaver (1949), "The Mathematical Theory of Communication", University of Illinois Press.

Bruce Tuckman & Mary Ann Jensen (1977), "Stages of small-group development revisited", Group & Organization Studies, Vol 2(4), pp 419–427.

UGLE (2020), "Constitutions of the Antient Fraternity of Free and Accepted Masons under the United Grand Lodge of England" (The Book of Constitutions), UGLE, London.

Acknowledgments

Throughout this book I have mentioned key steps along my own journey through Freemasonry. Here, I wish to thank and pay tribute to the various brethren who have been most instrumental in that journey. I hope the following will illustrate how what we do as experienced Freemasons can make a big difference to the lives and learning of others.

It took me five years to become a Freemason. I was very interested but unsure. W Bros. Ken Shaw, John Carvin (who became my proposer) and the late Kim Gale answered all the challenging questions I put to them, without ever pushing me. With their help, eventually my uncertainty gave way to decision, and I joined Pioneer Lodge. The result has been one of the most enjoyable and satisfying experiences of my life.

In my early years my mentors were W Bros. Alan Beckerton, the late Bill Summers and Steve Hilditch. From each of them, in different ways, I learned what it meant to be a member of a Lodge and gradually I began to make sense of what I had joined, its customs and its real meaning. They helped and supported me as I progressed through the various Lodge offices, into the chair and beyond.

Alan and I then became a strong double act, with me as Lodge Secretary and he as Director of Ceremonies in both Pioneer Lodge and Derby Lodge of Mark Master Masons. Ever since I have been convinced of the need for these two officers to work together very closely, to inject the underlying energy so evident in successful Lodges and to set the standards for others to follow. Assisted, of course, by others.

RW Bro. Graham Rudd, then the Provincial Grand Master for Derbyshire, and his Deputy, VW Bro. John Collison, opened the door into Provincial Freemasonry. Graham appointed me as Derbyshire's first

Provincial Grand Mentor, and later its Provincial Junior Grand Warden. As the Provincial Mentor, I quickly saw the relevance of my professional and Scouting experiences to situations within Freemasonry, so I adapted what I had learned elsewhere. Graham and John backed my efforts to promote a supportive, member-centric and needs based approach to mentoring. The result was a reduction in resignations within five years of Initiation from over 38% to 12.6%.

Graham also supported my wish to promote the relationship between Scouting and Freemasonry. He introduced me to the then Grand Secretary, RW Bro. Nigel Brown, who shared my view that there was a lot of potential for both organisations if we could build relationships and learn from each other. That is one of the central messages in my Prestonian Lecture and I have no doubt that Nigel played a key part in my appointment as the 2012 Prestonian Lecturer. I am grateful to his successors, RW Bro. Willie Shackell and RW Bro. David Staples, for continuing to support this work and for giving their time to meet senior colleagues in The Scout Association. I look forward to working with the new Grand Secretary, VW Bro. Adrian Marsh, to continue where they left off.

Around the time I first met the Grand Secretary, R.W.Bro. Bob Poxon asked me to be his Provincial Grand Secretary in the Mark Province of Derbyshire. This role taught me so much about managing Freemasonry at Provincial level, together with protocol and ceremonial matters. It also helped me develop my insights into what makes a Lodge successful or otherwise. As a Provincial ruler Bob was the epitome of warmth, clear principles, sound judgement, dignified bearing and good grace. He continues to be my Masonic role model, although I shall never match the example he set.

At one of the official deliveries of my Prestonian Lecture I met VW Bro. Mike Woodcock, then the President of the Royal Masonic Trust for Girls and Boys (RMTGB). Mike invited me to become involved in the Trust. I had spent some years as a Charity Steward and had been Director of Communications for Derbyshire's 2014 Festival, so I was very interested in getting more involved in the Masonic charities. I became a Council Member of the RMTGB, and helped develop its Communications and Fundraising strategy. On behalf of the RMTGB, I was involved in the work to consolidate the various charities into one and was nominated to become one the first Trustees of the Masonic Charitable Foundation (MCF). The first chair of the MCF, RW Bro. James Newman, steered the creation of the new entity with great skill and taught me much about charity governance.

When UGLE set up its Membership Focus Group (MFG), Nigel Brown asked me to join one of the sub-groups. As part of that work, I proposed the creation of a "Pathway into membership". This was enthusiastically received by the chair of the MFG, RW Bro. Ray Reed, Past Provincial Grand Master for Buckinghamshire, the then Deputy President of the Board of General Purposes. Ray asked me to develop the idea and to run a pilot study. W Bro. Shawn Christie, Assistant Grand Secretary, and RW Bro. Stephen Blank, then Provincial Grand Master for Cheshire, were particularly helpful as I developed the materials. That it was adopted by Grand Lodge was down to the guidance and commitment of RW Bros. Sir David Wootton, then Assistant Grand Master, Stephen Blank and Peter Taylor, then Provincial Grand Master for Shropshire, all of whom have been very supportive of me personally, especially as I tried to navigate my way around the heady heights of UGLE and its workings.

Bringing my journey to the present day, I wish to thank the two Provincial Grand Masters who appointed me to my current roles, RW Bros. Mark Estaugh (West Kent) and Philip Marshall (Nottinghamshire), both of whom have placed their confidence in me and put up with me in equal measure.

I thank the Deputy Grand Master, RW Bro. Sir David Wootton, who kindly wrote the foreword to this book. Sir David has always received my ideas and proposals with patience and good grace. I am very grateful for his support for this book. I hope it will provide our warranted Lodges with a means to make the changes that will secure their future.

I thank W Bro. Gerald Sclater, for bringing the words to life by producing the illustrations in this book, and W Bro. Martin Faulks and his team at Lewis Masonic, for taking it to market. Martin stuck with the idea for seven-habits, allowed me to delay its creation while I worked on the development of the Members' Pathway and has turned the words on my screen into the book in your hands.

Finally, I thank my wife, Diane, and daughter, Caroline, for allowing me to devote time to Freemasonry, for supporting me in all my activities and for always being there for me. Without their selfless love I would not be able to pursue my interests, let alone write about them.

There are of course others who have helped in various ways. I wish to pay especial tribute to all the Lodge and Chapter officers who have supported me in my learning, gradual understanding and progression in different Orders and degrees. By far the majority of these have set a great example and have passed on to their successors something that was better as a result of their enthusiasm, commitment and hard work.

All the above have been patient with me (not an easy task) and have nurtured my talents and ideas. Not a single one has ever sought to dampen my enthusiasm. I shall forever be grateful to them and to all the other brethren who have been part of my own journey through Freemasonry. May they be a shining example to the rest of us.

The Author

Tony Harvey has been a Freemason for over thirty years and has been the Master or equivalent "a number of times" in the Craft, Royal Arch and Mark and two other Orders. As well as being a Lodge Secretary and Charity Steward, he has held Provincial roles in the secretarial, membership, mentoring, learning & development, charity and communication areas of Freemasonry.

Professionally, Tony is a coach, speaker and consultant specialising in leadership, change and organisational development. His published books and articles focus on his own model of personal and organisational change, the Success Cycle. He holds degrees in psychology & education and in management and is a Fellow of the Learning & Performance Institute (FLPI), the Chartered Management Institute (FCMI), the Chartered Institute of Personnel & Development (FCIPD) and of the Royal Society of Arts (FRSA). He is an Associate Fellow of the Royal Historical Society.

Tony also has extensive experience of volunteer development within The Scouts, having helped that organisation develop its very successful "6-steps to adult recruitment", its adult training scheme and its model for leadership & management. He continues his active involvement in Scouting as a Training Manager in Derbyshire and an HQ Training Adviser with The Scout Association. He has received two awards for specially distinguished service to Scouting.

Tony has been appointed to several Masonic lectureships, including the Prestonian Lecture in 2012 with, "Scouting and Freemasonry: two parallel organisations?", which he has delivered on more than 130 occasions in every Province in England & Wales and to a number of overseas Districts and foreign Grand Lodges. During the Covid-19 pandemic he delivered online talks on more than 140 occasions for hosts on six continents.

Tony's writing and talks combine historical analysis with an understanding of organisational development to promote a forward-thinking approach to Freemasonry, based on the evolution of our Lodge practices while retaining our fundamental meaning and purpose.

Tony conceived, and between 2015 and 2020 was the main author of, United Grand Lodge of England's Members' Pathway, which the Past Pro Grand Master described as a "game changer."

Tony holds the ranks of Past Junior Grand Deacon (PJGD) in the United Grand Lodge of England, Past Assistant Grand Director of Ceremonies (PAGDC) in the Supreme Grand Chapter of England, Past Grand Junior Overseer (P.G.J.O.) in the Grand Lodge of Mark Master Masons and is also a grand officer in two other Orders within English Freemasonry. He is currently the Provincial Grand Membership Officer in Nottinghamshire and the Head of Learning & Development in West Kent.

You can find out more about Tony and his work on his professional website, https://tonyharvey.online and on his Masonic website, https://prestonian2012.com. He would like to receive short descriptions of how Lodges have used the seven habits to transform their health and strength, with a view to compiling a follow-up volume showcasing their stories. He also welcomes invitations to deliver talks from recognised Masonic organisations in all time zones. Tony can be contacted via his websites.